D0469923

Learning from the Best

Learning
from the
Best

Growing Greatness
in the Christian School

Gene Frost

ACSI.

Learning from the Best: Growing Greatness in the Christian School
by Gene Frost

ISBN 0-87463-160-2

© 2007 by Gene Frost
All rights reserved

This publication or parts thereof may not be reproduced in any form or by any means without written permission from the publisher.

CHRISTIAN SCHOOLS INTERNATIONAL (CSI)
3350 East Paris Ave. SE
Grand Rapids, MI 49512-3054

and

ASSOCIATION OF CHRISTIAN SCHOOLS INTERNATIONAL (ACSI)
731 Chapel Hill Drive
Colorado Springs, CO 80920

Printed in the United States of America

10 9 8 7 6 5 4 3 2 1

This book is dedicated to my parents
Dr. Eugene A. Frost, Sr. and Marie Frost
who sacrificed greatly to provide a Christian school education
for their five children.

Contents

Acknowledgments

As in most large undertakings there are many organizations and people to thank.

The sponsors...
• My good friend and mentor Scott Bolinder, who as Executive VP and publisher of Zondervan, made the original introduction to Zondervan's research department. They not only recognized the good this study could do for their customers but also its benefit for encouraging good within the body of Christ. Zondervan of Grand Rapids, Michigan then became the primary sponsor of this study.
• My second sponsor was the Wheaton Academy Institute, which is dedicated to promoting great Christian education. The Institute handled all the infrastructure, accounting, and support necessary to make this study possible.

The research advisory team...
Several educational leaders provided insight in the design phase of this study by serving as my study advisory team. Each member gave me invaluable insight and encouragement as I put this study together. The members of the team were: Dr. Jim Drexler, chair of the Education Department at Covenant College, Lookout Mountain, GA; Dr. Rani Mathai, associate professor of education at Judson College, Elgin, IL; and Dr. David Roth, Chief Education Officer, Wheaton Academy Virtual, West Chicago, IL.

The visiting team members...
Several good friends accompanied me on various campus visits and provided an extra pair of eyes and ears that helped me to understand what I was observing and discovering. They were Rob Keith, Jim Long, Joe Chisholm, Peter Baur, and Tom Paulsen.

The schools...
Each of the schools that participated in this study was exceedingly gracious in providing hospitality and transparency to me and my team members. I

was able to make many friends on each campus. I would like to particularly thank each administrator, staff member, teacher, parent and student who took the time to speak with us, fill out our surveys, etc. Many will be mentioned or alluded to in the pages of this book, many are not, but all are very much appreciated. I could not have asked for a more cooperative response and I'm looking for great things for each of these schools.

The editorial team...
• My administrative assistant Pippa Bellis, who made so many of the travel arrangements, collated copies and synthesized countless pages of data.
• My primary typist and moral support, Barbara Frost, who translated all my handwritten drafts into a readable copy. She has had nearly 30 years of experience, having been my loving friend and encouraging wife all that time.
• My good friends Gary Gnidovic and John Wilson. Gary used his award-winning skill in developing the cover art, book layout and design. John provided the book's title along with strategic advice and counsel out of his vast experience as editor of *Books and Culture*, a magazine from Christianity Today International.
• The professional assistance and editing of Randy and Jeron Frame. Randy is publications director for Palmer Seminary, PA and Jeron is an award-winning children's author. These friends along with the publishing team at CSI helped to polish the original manuscript into a final coherent work.

The inspiration...
Finally, I would like to thank Jim Collins who has inspired so much good work in the not-for-profit sector and who inspired in part my pursuit of this project.

The publishers...
Both Christian School International (CSI) and Association of Christian Schools International (ACSI) worked together in the publishing of this book so that it could have the widest possible distribution and help the many schools that would be receptive to the concepts and lessons shared.

Introduction

A Note to the Reader about Jim Collins' Book *Good to Great*

The first half of this book uses some of the concepts from Jim Collins' best-selling book *Good to Great*. While Collins gleaned his concepts from studying great companies, this book will apply those same principles to the running of great schools.

Although this book will briefly describe Collins' concepts, I believe readers would also greatly benefit from reading *Good to Great* and Jim Collins' monograph *Good to Great and the Social Sectors*. (This latter work discusses the good-to-great concepts in the non-profit setting.) All in-text page citations, unless otherwise noted, reference *Good to Great*, published by HarperCollins, 2001.

The Selected Concepts and Scope of the Study

Six of Collins' good-to-great concepts (Level 5 Leadership; First Who, Then What; Confronting the Brutal Facts; Hedgehog Concept; Technology as Accelerator; and The Flywheel) will be discussed in chapters 2 through 7. This study is not intended to be an exhaustive evaluation of Collins' concepts or a complete application of these concepts to Christian secondary schools. But first we will show how the six concepts readily correlate to the successful running of a great Christian secondary school. Second, we will describe what a great Christian school looks like using a composite picture of seven comprehensively studied schools.

It is hoped that this study will not only encourage healthy practices in Christian schools but will also stimulate thinking on how those of us involved in Christian education might continue to build our own models of greatness.

SCHOOLS THAT ARE GROWING GREATNESS

A narrative study of some of the concepts

highlighted by Jim Collins in his book Good to Great

as they are demonstrated in great Christian secondary schools.

The seven comprehensive schools studied were:

Annapolis Area Christian School, Severn, Maryland;

Bellevue Christian High School, Clyde Hill, Washington;

Cincinnati Hills Christian Academy, Cincinnati, Ohio;

First Presbyterian Day School, Macon, Georgia;

The King's Academy, West Palm Beach, Florida;

Westminster Christian Academy, St. Louis, Missouri;

Wheaton Academy, West Chicago, Illinois.

CHAPTER 1

The Search for Greatness

Identifying Best Practices

What does it take to be great? Why do so few institutions achieve greatness? In his book *Good to Great* Jim Collins explains that there are so few great institutions because there are so many good institutions. In the opening lines of his bestseller Collins declares, "We don't have great schools, principally because we have good schools. We don't have great government, principally because we have good government. Few people attain great lives, in large part because it is just so easy to settle for a good life. The vast majority of companies never become great, precisely because the vast majority become quite good—and that is their main problem" (page 1).

I found it interesting that Jim Collins' first example was of schools. Schools then were the subject of the original Zondervan "Growing Greatness in Christian Schools" study and this resulting book. This book attempts to answer the question "What does it take to become a 'great school,' and more specifically, a 'great Christian secondary school?'"

A Lifelong Search

My lifelong passion has been to move Christian education from good to great. I can remember back to my days as a student in a Christian high school and saying, "If only they would let the students run the school, we'd make it great." Then as a teacher I said, "If only they would do this or that, then we'd be a great school." Finally as a board member I was challenged to make policy decisions that did, in fact, affect the course of the school. As a board member at Wheaton Academy I saw the enrollment grow from 205 to 565 over a 15-year period—pretty dramatic when the enrollment had been shrinking for the previous five years. Student satisfaction was up, teacher turnover was down, and success in extracurriculars and sports began to pour in. But were we great?

The board I was part of for a private company studied the book *Good to Great* by Jim Collins. As I read I asked myself, "How would Wheaton Academy measure up? Are we great? Are we good?"

Our company's executive team spent a day with Jim Collins in Colorado. During the breaks Jim talked about his interest in applying these principles to the social sectors. (He has since released his monograph *Good to Great and the Social Sectors*.) I continued to ask, "How would Wheaton Academy stack up to the concepts that Collins had outlined in this original work?" This book is an attempt to answer that question.

Collins' Concepts Applied to Good Schools

In his original research Collins was able to define "great" by measuring the economic success of various companies over time. His research isolated eleven companies that were able to make the leap from good to great and contrasted them with comparable companies that had failed to make the leap. Collins' *Good to Great* research team was then able to identify several factors that they believed could explain this leap, but this study's limited scope prevented it from comparing its identified good schools to a control group. Therefore, this work will assume that Collins' factors correlate with building a great institution, and I will simply attempt to apply six of those concepts to Christian secondary education. (See the chart at the end of this chapter for a simple synopsis of the six concepts that will be studied in this book.)

But how do we find great schools? Can we measure a school's success strictly in terms of economic outputs? The simple answer is that we can't. Collins recognized this problem when he wrote *Good to Great and the Social Sectors*. Here he explains that the not-for-profit must hold itself accountable for "progress in outputs even if those outputs defy measurement" (Monograph, page 5). Collins goes on to explain, "It doesn't really matter whether you can quantify your results. What matters is that you rigorously assemble evidence—quantitative or qualitative—to track your progress. If the evidence is primarily qualitative, think like a trial lawyer assembling the combined body of evidence. If the evidence is primarily quantitative, then think of yourself as a laboratory scientist assembling and assessing the data" (Monograh, page 7).

As a good lawyer or scientist I set out to examine the evidence, but how was I to find and identify great schools?

In Search of Great Christian Secondary Schools

In order to answer the question "Do great Christian secondary schools correlate with Jim Collins' good-to-great concepts?" I had to identify some great schools. This would not be easy; there are no simple economic matrices such as stock price and dividends to judge a school's performance, so I was limited to a subjective measure of outputs. How could I do this? I decided to contact the major associations in which private Christian high schools were members. I approached the Association of Christian Schools International; Christian Schools International; Association of Lutheran Secondary Schools; Seventh Day Adventist North American Office of Education; National Catholic Educational Association; PAIDEIA, Inc. (a think tank of Christian preparatory schools); and the National Association of Episcopal Schools. All but the Episcopal association chose to participate. I asked each association to suggest schools that they believed would be appropriate for the study. The criteria were simply that these be secondary schools with an enrollment of over 300, exemplify qualities of greatness in the eyes of the association, and be interested in doing the work necessary to participate in the study. The various associations submitted the names of more than 100 schools. The research team selected twelve of these schools for study based on significant growth in size, budget, and/or accomplishments of the school's mission demonstrated by best practices and the school's willingness to participate.

The original plan was to study the ten most promising applicants, but the applications revealed too many schools doing great things. It was decided that the twelve selected schools would be divided into two groups—seven would be considered for the comprehensive study of the six good-to-great concepts, and five would be studied for particular best practices that resulted in part from their being a great school. The following schools were chosen:

Comprehensively Studied Schools:
Annapolis Area Christian School, Severn, Maryland
Bellevue Christian High School, Clyde Hill, Washington
Cincinnati Hills Christian Academy, Cincinnati, Ohio
First Presbyterian Day School, Macon, Georgia
The King's Academy, West Palm Beach, Florida
Westminster Christian Academy, St. Louis, Missouri
Wheaton Academy, West Chicago, Illinois

Best Practice Schools:
Catholic Central High School, Grand Rapids, Michigan
Evangelical Christian School, Cordova, Tennessee
Lutheran High School North, Macomb, Michigan
Lynden Christian High School, Lynden, Washington
Xavier College Preparatory, Phoenix, Arizona

The school's full name will appear when necessary for clarity; otherwise the abbreviated name or initials will be used. All administrative names are actual, but the names of all others (teachers, board members, parents, students, etc.) have been changed and their identities altered.

This book has been divided into three parts. The first section reflects the seven schools that participated in the comprehensive study that attempts to relate Collins' good-to-great concepts to schools. In order to do this, a survey designed to test for the prevalence of good-to-great concepts was administered to the entire school faculty and administration. A parent satisfaction survey and a leadership evaluation survey were also administered. A number of interviews were conducted with various school constituencies, including teachers, administrators, students, parents, and board members. The result of the study of these seven schools is covered in chapters 2 through 7.

The second section of this book summarizes best practices demonstrated by the five remaining schools. These best practices are believed to have grown out of running an excellent school; we hope that these stories will serve as examples of what a great school can accomplish.

The appendices include a summary of the survey findings. It is hoped that this study will encourage further exploration and discussion about what makes a great school as well as a great Christian institution. Both the parent satisfaction and the Growing Greatness surveys are available for other schools to administer (see the appendices for details).

The Spiritual Dimension and Other Applications

Narrow study category notwithstanding, I trust that this book will be valuable to many. There is immediate application not only to all Christian schools but also other non-profit organizations, such as public schools, churches, charities, and service organizations. Those involved in various not-for-profits can find value as they apply good-to-great concepts to their world.

A word of clarification is needed in regard to the spiritual nature of the task and goals of running a Christian school. Everything that a Christian school does has a spiritual dimension. Jesus reminds us that apart from Him we can do nothing (John 15:5). Apart from the Spirit of God at work in a school, nothing of lasting value will be accomplished spiritually there. But in keeping with the axiom that "all truth is God's truth," the research world has many truths to offer that can be applied to the practice and discipline of running a Christian school. To the degree that any practice is true it can provide a vehicle for the Spirit to work. This book will not attempt to build a theological basis for the good-to-great concepts but rather seek to discover how they may be applied to the goal of creating and administrating great Christian secondary schools in which God may be able to work. In the words of Randy Brunk, Head of School at Cincinnati Hills Christian School, "I do not separate the secular from the sacred. Everything is God's, and it is all sacred to me." Let's take a look together and see what we can learn.

A Brief Primer of Six of Collins' Good-to-Great Principles found in his book *Good to Great*

Level 5 Leadership—Unlike the traditional picture of the up-front, assertive charismatic leader (think George Patton and Donald Trump), leaders who brought their companies from good to great blended personal humility and unrelenting determination. They consistently gave away all the credit and accepted all the blame as they led their companies to greatness.

First Who, Then What—Conventional wisdom is to first lay out a plan and then find the right people to execute the plan. Collins discovered that great plans come only when you get great people. The right people—the "who"—come first. They will then make the "what"—the right plans.

Confronting the Brutal Facts—The mantra in many organizations is to stay positive. But too often that attitude allows for glossing over bad news that needs to be addressed. Collins discovered that only when you listen to the bad news, take it seriously, and deal with it without focusing on blame can you find an answer that will not only solve the problem but lead to success.

The Hedgehog Concept—Business success is often linked to the flashy and powerful. The lion, eagle, and cobra are all common symbols for cunning, power, and effectiveness. But Collins selects the hedgehog for his picture. The hedgehog does one thing really well, and it thwarts its enemies every time: it rolls up into a ball and exposes its sharp quills. According to Collins, the good-to-great company has an uncanny knack for knowing what it is good at and sticking to it. Collins probed deeper and discovered that the thing good-to-great companies were really good at (their "hedgehog principle") was actually the intersection or overlap of three very different things: what they were most passionate about, what they were better than anyone else at doing, and what they could make money doing. If you are passionate about something that you're very good at and you can make money doing it, you have a hedgehog principle.

Technology Accelerators—Collins distinguishes between technology that creates momentum and technology that accelerates momentum. The former is short-lived and often creates the kind of change we saw in the dot com bubble—that which was easily replaced by the next technological breakthrough. On the other hand, using technology as a tool to accelerate the momentum already created by a solid hedgehog concept leads to enduring change.

The Flywheel—Like a giant flywheel, the good-to-great companies that Collins studied spent a lot of time early on just trying to get rolling. Thanks to unrelenting pressure (continuing to do the right things), the wheel began to turn over time until it became nearly unstoppable. This analogy seemed to explain the success curve of the good-to-great companies.

CHAPTER 2

The Christian Concept of "Servant Leadership"

Level 5 Leadership

"**E**verything rises and falls with leadership." So says church leadership expert John Maxwell on his Maximum Impact website (www.maximumimpact.com). The good-to-great concepts recognize this as well by affirming that an organization, whether a business or a school, can rise only as high as its leadership allows. As I read Jim Collins' definition of a Level 5 leader—one who "builds enduring greatness through a paradoxical blend of personal humility and professional will" (page 20)—I thought of all the explicitly Christian definitions of leadership I have heard and read. Isn't Collins describing the "servant leader" of the Christian tradition? In fact, Collins had entertained calling his Level 5 leader a "servant leader," but his research team objected because the term sounded "weak or meek" (page 30). As believers, however, we are led by the example of Christ, who was indeed meek but was certainly not weak. Although his team shunned the term, Collins' Level 5 leader is an apt description of "servant leadership" as outlined in Scripture and Christian literature.

The question for this study remains: "Were these the kind of leaders in charge of the Growing Greatness schools?"

Level 5 Leadership

Between January and May of 2006, my various visiting research partners and I conducted a twelve-school tour during which we interviewed the heads of each school. First on our list was Randy Brunk, Head of School at Cincinnati Hills Christian Schools. (Randy had rejected the title of "headmaster" out of a concern that it communicates too much of an authoritarian form of leadership, not to mention his concern for the sensitivities in a border state that still deals with the ramifications of a history that featured masters and slaves.)

When my visiting research partner Rob Keith and I asked Randy about his leadership style, he stepped out from behind his desk to sit and talk with us, an action that clearly was consistent with his perspective. "I'm a listener," he said. "I listen, listen, listen. If you understand what a person is trying to say, you can often work out a win-win solution. Often it's just a matter of timing or perspective. But unless you make sure that the person you're talking to feels heard and understood, you're just inviting conflict."

In addition to listening, Randy cited the importance of delegating: "I try to limit the decisions made in this office. I try to make sure that as many decisions as possible are pushed down to those who report to me so that they and their teams can show leadership. We try to find champions around here and then let them run. If I'm involved in everything, I dis-empower everybody else.

"Of course I'm willing to step in if something is broken, but I try to be careful to do it through the appropriate channels and not to embarrass my staff and teachers."

When we asked Randy about his weaknesses as a leader, he quickly cited two: "I'm too focused on wanting people to be happy, and I'm too helpful at times. In the first case I've learned to just simply tell the truth and not lead people on, hoping my answer will make them feel better. Secondly, I've learned that being too helpful can be very dis-empowering for the person you're trying to help.

"I believe that the greatest thing I've learned about leadership is that I need to keep learning. The minute you think you have arrived, you're in trouble." Then he added, "I think I've learned from every conversation I've ever been in."

One of the things Randy has learned is how to address situations in which people are upset. His advice: "Don't be offended. Keep listening, and try to understand what is behind their seeming attack. When parents are on the edge of their seats, I let them talk. When they sit back in their seats, then it's my turn to talk. I make sure to let the parents know that I care about their child. This is number one with them."

The more we talked with Randy, the more we recognized that he modeled many of the traits of a Level 5 leader, as defined by Collins. But was he the exception or the rule? Through our survey instruments and personal interviews with heads of the other 11 schools, we eventually concluded that a majority of our Growing Greatness school leaders clearly demonstrated most of the eight identified traits of Level 5 leadership. Two survey instruments seemed to verify our observations. First was the self-measurement and evaluation measurements based on the eight Collins' good-to-great leadership traits (see chart below).

Summary: The Two Sides of Level 5 Leadership outlined by Jim Collins in *Good to Great* (page 36)

Professional Will	**Personal Humility**
Creates superb results, a clear catalyst in the transition from good to great.	Demonstrates a compelling modesty, shunning public adulation; never boastful.
Demonstrates an unwavering resolve to do whatever must be done to produce the best long-term results, no matter how difficult.	Acts with quiet, calm determination; relies principally on inspired standards, not inspiring charisma, to motivate.
Sets the standard of building an enduring great company; will settle for nothing less.	Channels ambition into the company, not the self; sets up successors for even greater success in the next generation.
Looks in the mirror, not out the window, to apportion responsibility for poor results, never blaming other people, external factors, or bad luck.	Looks out the window, not in the mirror, to apportion credit for the success of the company—to other people, external factors, and good luck.

The school leaders we surveyed consistently rated high on both self-assessment and peer and subordinate evaluations. (Appendix 2 includes a more detailed summary of our findings.)

Let's now look at a few of the strongest examples of leaders who demonstrated the dual qualities of personal humility and professional will.

Humility and Will

One of the challenges of interviewing the heads of schools was that they were so willing to give away all the credit for everything the school had accomplished. It was very difficult to get Gregg Thompson, Headmaster at First Presbyterian Day School in Macon, Georgia, to talk about himself. When pressed on how he had created such a strong school, he would offer genuine responses such as, "God's in control," "God gets all the credit," or "My success here is due to bringing on a great staff and letting them build a great school."

This humility was confirmed by observations from board members ("He is a servant leader"), from parents ("Gregg is so in tune with the students and teachers that my jaw dropped"), and from teachers ("Gregg always finds a way to thank us for everything we do").

But it was not just his humility that stood out—it was also his determined will that First Presbyterian be excellent. This determination was displayed in part during Gregg's interview before he was hired. The board members had found that Gregg was the only candidate who thoroughly believed that a school could be both distinctively Christian and programmatically excellent. In fact, Gregg had insisted that being a thoroughly Christian school demands excellence. Indeed, excellence has become a word that Gregg uses frequently, and one of his teachers cited excellence as Gregg's defining focus.

Gregg's determined will far transcended talk. He evaluated the school's needs and decided that First Presbyterian needed a full-time curriculum director. His decision to hire Barry Shealy was not a popular one. Veteran teachers saw no need to rework their classes or have someone tell them what and how to teach. Although the faculty wasn't happy with Gregg's decision, he calmly pushed ahead. Now, several years later, the faculty is nearly unanimous that Barry has been instrumental in aligning the curriculum to a distinctive and articulate Christian worldview.

Gregg's focus on excellence has raised the bar for the entire school. "He's supportive, but he also holds people accountable," explained an upper school teacher. Faculty evaluations are rigorous. Student outputs are closely measured. Excellence is being sought throughout the curriculum and the extracurricular activities.

This combination of personal humility and professional will has won the day at First Presbyterian, which is reaping the benefits of a Level 5 leader who is seeking to enable the school to accomplish its mission not by pushing himself to the front and dragging others along but rather by recognizing the gifts and abilities of his reports and encouraging them to move forward with him.

Growing from Within and Succession

One surprising observation from *Good to Great* is that almost all of the good to great companies Collins studied grew the senior leader from within. Realizing that the pool of senior executive candidates is relatively low in most Christian schools, I expected to find very little promotion of leadership from within. Of the twenty heads of school and/or principals included in this study, however, fourteen of them were promoted from within the existing school or related school system.

These leaders were in turn strongly focused on growing the next generation of leadership—what Collins calls "setting up successors for success" (page 25). A perfect example is Jim Marsh, Head of School at Westminster Christian Academy in St. Louis. My research associate Jim Long and I asked a group of veteran our standard question: "What are the three things that have moved this school from 'good' to 'great'?" The first answer came instantly: "Hiring Jim Marsh." We had already heard from administrators, board members, and parents what a wonderful leader Jim Marsh was. Now we were hearing it again from the teachers. I asked what made Jim such an effective leader.

"He's a quiet, humble leader," said one teacher. "He sets high expectations but you want to succeed for him."

23

"Jim makes the tough decisions. He's raised the bar and removed those who didn't make it over the bar," explained another. "He always puts the teacher front and center. He knows that the accomplishment of our mission is based on the success of the teacher, and he supports our success." High praise from those down the chain of command!

We had only had a short, friendly conversation with Jim when he picked us up from the nearby airport, so during the day we had to put together the puzzle pieces to form a picture of his leadership. He emerged as a clear example of a combination of professional will and personal humility. But he had been in this role for over twenty years. We wondered how this leadership developed. By the end of the day the pieces were beginning to fit.

According to Collins, there is no lack of potential for Level 5 leadership. The failure lies in developing potential leaders. Jim Marsh is an example of someone who has grown over time into a full Level 5 leader. One administrator mentioned an early meeting after Jim had arrived on campus. The school was struggling financially and was badly in need of better facilities, but in spite of these pressing demands the administrative leadership knew that a vision and academic plan would be necessary in order for the school to succeed. Jim asked the senior team to write up the plan. The team told Jim that they couldn't do it. They needed his expertise and leadership to craft these defining documents.

Jim was willing to pull the load himself if necessary. We were told, "Jim worked well into the night pecking away on his typewriter to help build a plan that we all could get behind." Thus as a young administrator who was growing into his potential as a Level 5 leader, Jim learned to negotiate the fine balance between delegating and doing some of the hard things himself.

Jim himself told us the story of his first fundraiser—a story he'd waited ten years to tell anyone else. Jim and his team had worked tirelessly on the school's first big fundraising banquet. The dinner was a success. Jim lingered outside the banquet hall talking to parents and constituents for nearly an hour afterwards. When he went back into the dining room to collect the checks and pledges left on the tables, he discovered to his horror that the tables had been cleared and the hall was empty! Long into the night Jim and his assistant combed through the dumpster to recover these crucial gifts. Not wanting to offend the donors, Jim told no one about his heroic "midnight dumpster diving" until many years later. He was learning not only the importance of tending to details but also that the highs and lows of leadership have to be taken in stride.

We were interested in the board's frustration with Jim's continuing to bring up the matter of succession planning. The board, of course, would like Jim to stay as long as possible, but, like a true Level 5 leader, Jim wants to plan for his successor's success. Having reached the age of sixty, he believes that a viable plan should be put in place for the good of the organization. Unfortunately it's more common for the board to bring up the topic of succession for an administrator approaching retirement age.

The board had also been frustrated by Jim's declining of raises and deferred compensation when Jim thought that the school couldn't afford it. I wondered, "Would I want to work for this person?" You bet I would. The puzzle pieces were in place. Westminster Christian Academy had grown a wonderful example of a Level 5 leader who is busy growing the next generation of leadership.

Great leaders realize that they cannot run a great school without great people. With that in mind, we now turn to the next good-to-great principle: Find the right people and put them in the right positions.

CHAPTER 3

The Importance of the Teacher in the Christian School Enterprise

First Who, Then What

Christian organizations and non-profits in general often fall victim to the "volunteer syndrome." If someone is willing to work for long hours and low wages and feels "called" to the work, who are we to turn them away? Jesus, however, used very high standards to select His followers. The rich young ruler in the New Testament (Mark 10:17–22) looked like a very good candidate for membership on Jesus' team. He had kept all the law, he was looking for someone to follow and, he was extremely wealthy. Jesus, however, sent the rich young ruler away because he didn't measure up to Jesus' high demands. (I would have been tempted at least to invite this volunteer to serve on the development committee of my not-for-profit organization.)

If it's true that an organization will rise no higher than its leadership, then it is equally true that the excellence of an organization's product cannot exceed the excellence of those responsible for producing that product. For the Christian school this means that the school will never be any better than its teachers and staff.

This painful truth faced Dr. David Roth and his board during the second year of David's tenure as headmaster of Wheaton Academy. The new purpose statement for the school stated that Wheaton Academy seeks "to nurture growth through excellence, relationships and service all to the glory of God." The school's decline in the years before David's arrival was due largely to the fact that very little excellence, quality relationships, or even service was going on. David and his principal, Jon Keith, had just concluded an evaluation of the teachers. They had built a simple grid scoring each teacher on a scale of 1–3 in each of the three focus areas of the vision statement: excellence, relationships, and service. They had employed simple definitions and corresponding questions for each focus area. Excellence was defined as excellence in the classroom. Was this person a great teacher? Relationship was narrowed down to the relationship between the teacher and the student. Does this teacher love his or her students, and do the students know it? Service was defined as having a servant's heart. Is this person willing to come early and stay late when necessary?

The reality was that five of the fifteen teachers were failing in one or more of the categories. They had been warned after David's first year that this was unacceptable, but now after the second year their evaluations seemed largely unchanged. These five teachers would not be extended new contracts. David had just fired one-third of his teaching staff! What would happen next?

The Transformation of Finding the Right People

The anticipated trauma ensued. Several of the teachers had a small but vocal following. It was difficult not to respond in kind to the accusations being hurled at the administration. (One crucial point is that David was seen as a Level 5 leader. He had not only served two years as head of Wheaton Academy but had served successfully for twenty years as principal of Wheaton Christian Grammar School. His ability to weather this storm successfully was rooted in part in the credibility he had taken years to earn.)

Wheaton Academy set out to recruit the best possible teachers they could find. They advertised nationally through lengthy ads in *Christianity Today* and *WORLD* magazine, two of the most widely read magazines within the Christian evangelical world. They set aside a recruiting budget and a part-time staff position to pursue and process applications. What was once a recruiting process that had the administration scrambling to fill teacher positions in August was replaced by a timely review of hundreds of applicants and even a waiting list of able teachers in certain departments.

The results were dramatic. Attendance almost tripled in the next fifteen years. Wheaton Academy calls its great teachers "living curriculum teachers." When Jon Keith, principal at Wheaton Academy, first asked the faculty to help describe what the school would want and not want in a living curriculum teacher, midway through the exercise one teacher protested the emerging list: "You'd have to be Jesus to do that!" Jon paused and then responded, "I think you're getting it!" Wheaton Academy is looking for Christ-like models for their students—teachers who reflect the school's mission for excellence, relationships, and service.

This change has had "the most dramatic effect in transforming Wheaton Academy," says Jon. "Before, the administration spent 80 percent of its time solving problems caused by teachers. Now we can spend that time finding quality teachers."

Jon continues, "The resulting culture is one where kids can flourish. We try to treat kids as more mature than their age, and in most cases they rise to that level. We also try to release kids to lead. We understand that this is a learning process for kids and that sometimes they will fail, but that is how they learn. In fact, if there is not enough failing going on then there is probably not enough freedom."

My research assistant Tom Paulsen saw this culture at work in the Zambia Project, a WA student-led response to the AIDS pandemic in Zambia. The students have raised over $400,000 during the past four years. This project has included multiple student mission trips to the Kakolo Village community, where their resources have made possible the building of a school, Wheaton Academy Zambia, and a medical clinic. The senior farewell chapel highlighted this culture with a multimedia presentation, a video, and a band performance, all designed and run completely by the students. Jon explains that the class sponsors provide the guardrails so the students can't run off the road but that the school clearly wants the students behind the wheel as they navigate their high school experiences.

This empowering of teachers in order to empower students takes Collins' concept one step further down the chain of command and creates a tremendously dynamic learning culture. This job of finding the right teachers and staff is one Collins refers to as "getting the right people on the bus" and is a key driver for greatness. My notes confirmed that finding the right teachers and plugging them into the right jobs was a universal constant for all our Growing Greatness schools.

Getting the Right People on the Bus

"Finding great teachers is Job One," said Ron Taylor, superintendent of Bellevue Christian Schools. "What matters most is what happens between the teacher and student when the teacher closes the door. That's why it is so important to not only find the right teachers but to work with them and train them for maximum effectiveness." New teachers are paid to attend Bellevue's two-day summer orientation for new teachers in order to emphasize the importance of this orientation to the school's mission. Gregg Thompson, Headmaster at First Presbyterian Day School, summarized a key step in accomplishing his school's mission: Attract and retain the right teachers and staff.

Administrators weren't the only ones articulating this principle; teachers themselves pinpointed the need for good hiring practices. One teacher at Cincinnati Hills explained, "The key is hiring great teachers and setting high standards for them." Her colleague added, "The school has made a huge effort to hire qualified, great teachers."

The students in all our Growing Greatness schools recognize this when they listed teachers even ahead of peers and friends as what they appreciated most about their schools. A parent from Wheaton Academy told me that his daughter had explained how different her college friends' high school experiences had been from hers. "We had a college writing assignment where you were supposed to talk about your most significant relationship with a teacher in high school. Most of the students in my class couldn't think of one. My problem was I couldn't pick only one because I had so many."

Students repeatedly spoke of having teachers' phone numbers in their cell phones, the discipling breakfasts, the accountability groups, the emails, the encouragements, the tough love, the friendships, the camaraderie, the coaching, the learning outside of class that all come from a significant relationship with a teacher.

After hearing so many students talk about the importance of their teachers, I recalled the original test that David Roth and Jon Keith scribbled out fifteen years ago: "Do they love kids? Are they excellent teachers? Are they willing to come early and stay late when necessary?" That's still a pretty good description of who you want on the bus.

Getting the Wrong People off the Bus

The difficulty of getting the wrong people off the bus is universally recognized. Many admitted that they had moved too slowly and, in an attempt to be nice, had only prolonged bad situations and sometimes even made them worse. Two strategies emerged as proactive ways to ensure that the right people were kept on the bus and in the right seats.

First, high standards, rigorous accountability, and evaluation are necessary. Student evaluations enhance the evaluation process. Every school that used student evaluations believed that they were the best barometer of what was actually happening in the classroom when the teacher closed the door.

Second, in several schools a positive attitude toward teacher turnover was beginning to emerge. Jon Keith explains this approach when he says, "We want teachers to work in their area of giftedness as believers. If we find that their gifts don't fit inside the school we want to find the place that those gifts can be used outside the school. We want what ultimately is best for the teacher as well as Wheaton Academy." Even with this positive outlook Jon admits, "It's still hard to do!"

Hard to do? Yes. Essential? Absolutely. The next chapter will describe the "what." It will lay out some of the ways the right team of administrators, teachers, and staff can tackle the task of educating Christian young people.

CHAPTER 4

Being Honest About the Difficulties

Confronting the Brutal Facts

One of the things that inspired Jim Collins to write *Good to Great* was an encounter he had over dinner with someone who had read his first bestseller, *Built to Last*. The dinner guest told Jim that of course the companies he had written about in *Built to Last* were great companies, but they seemed to have always been great companies. They had great histories, great leaders, and tremendous resources. But that was of little help to this dinner guest's not-so-great company, which seemed to possess none of the assets of the companies featured in *Built to Last*!

You may be having the same reaction to the schools in this study: "Of course we could be a great school if we had their enrollment, giving base, heritage, etc."

But one of the goals of this study was to select schools that have overcome difficult obstacles. Westminster came close to selling its building because of a lack of funds and students. Wheaton Academy came close to closing in the 1970s and faced 30 percent operating budget deficits as recently as the late 1980s. Cincinnati Hills faced a nearly million dollar shortfall because of the failure to reconcile its cash versus accrual system of bookkeeping. First Presbyterian Day School set out to compete with its neighboring preparatory schools only to be slapped by its accrediting agency for having inadequate scope and sequence, no meaningful staff development, and no uniform understanding of its own philosophy of Christian education. These difficulties seemed almost insurmountable hurdles for these schools.

We discovered that most of the schools in our study had to overcome difficulties as they grew. It is difficult for any organization to admit weaknesses and failures, and Christian schools are no different. Collins pointed out that all of the companies he studied faced problems (page 65ff). The difference was that the good-to-great companies were better at acknowledging, discussing, and dealing with them.

One school was almost lost by the wrong response to the brutal facts. The board thought that the Lord had led the right leader to their school. After all, he was the first head in their history with a doctorate. They committed to following him, staying "positive" all the way. The problem was that the facts were not positive. Instead of looking at declining enrollment as the school's problem, the board blamed the "baby bust" of the 80s. A board member should have pointed out that a 30 percent decline in enrollment cannot be attributed to the "baby bust!" But no one wanted to be negative. Key faculty leaving should have made someone ask, "Why?" or insist on exit interviews to find out what was making these teachers leave. Instead, the answer, "The Lord led them away," ended all inquiry. The growing budget deficit should have raised questions of why constituents were not giving. Instead, a "tough economy" was an answer that didn't ruffle any feathers.

Finally, a cadre of board members decided to face the brutal facts. They led efforts to apply the principles covered in chapters 2 and 3 of this book, resulting in a turnover in leadership and changes designed to put the right team in place. They also recognized the need to establish the right mission (which will be covered in the next chapter) and then to stay the course.

All this started with a willingness to face the brutal facts, to recognize a problem, and then to help solve the problem instead of denying it. Facing brutal facts is not the same as finding fault. Collins offers four constructive practices for facing and addressing the brutal facts:

1. Lead with questions, not answers.
2. Engage in dialogue and debate, not coercion.
3. Conduct autopsies without blame.
4. Build red-flag mechanisms that turn information into information that cannot be ignored.

A final ingredient that we need to recognize is the Holy Spirit's role as

we navigate these difficult issues. We are in constant need of God's leading and the presence of His Spirit to drive the enterprise of the Christian
school, but this need is never more apparent than when we face difficult
circumstances. In these times criticism and blame can easily replace the
inquiry and teamwork that are desperately needed in order to move
through complex times.

The Brutal Facts for The King's Academy

"Rely completely on God." This is the answer one board member gave to
one of my standard opening questions, "What are the most important
things you've done to move your school from good to great?" At first his
response seemed to be a mere cliché, but the earnestness with which he
answered suggested that there was a testimony behind his answer—a testimony to God's greatness in overcoming difficulties.

The location of The King's Academy was untenable; it was right next
to a growing international airport. Not only was the school landlocked by
the airport, but the ever increasing air traffic in West Palm Beach was
becoming a danger. Then the inevitable happened: a plane crashed across
the street from the school. "It could have hit one of the school buildings,"
thought president Jeffrey Loveland. "What parents want their children in
the flight pattern of an international airport?"

Perhaps the school needed to simply do the best it could with what it
had. After all, the cost of moving would be prohibitive. Such an approach,
however, would illustrate a lack of will or ability to confront the brutal
facts. Yes, the prospect of moving to a new location entailed questions and
uncertainties, but remaining in an increasingly dangerous location was
simply unthinkable.

The first decision was to continue to plan for growth on the present
site. Until the school could find an alternative site it had to respond to the
increasing demands for a Christian education and drew up plans for a
two-story building.

Although the school didn't know it at the time, its commitment to
continue to grow and build became the catalyst for the school's move. The
county saw the plans and decided to buy the school out of its land. They

approached the school with a generous offer for its land and buildings; now the school had to find a new property.

Encouraged by these developments, The King's Academy began to search for space for the school. Finding adequate land at a reasonable price in West Palm Beach, Florida, was no easy task. Many of the possibilities were too expensive, and several other potential deals seemed to fall apart at the last moment.

Once again, when it looked like the school would be unable to move, the Lord moved the county to step in. The county owned a large parcel that included unbuildable wetland and open spaces, which would be ideal for sports fields with enough buildable acres for the new school. Would this be the solution that the school's leadership and families had prayed so long for? One hurdle remained: county approval of the land swap and cash payment.

Finally the land swap that would give The King's Academy 60 acres of new land and $8.5 million to use toward its new building was going to be put to a vote by the county commissioners. A close vote was anticipated. Then calamity struck. A few days before the vote, the morning edition of the *Palm Beach Post* accused The King's Academy of double-dealing. The paper alleged that the school had received a "sweetheart deal" and that the county was giving away the land at a below-market price. The school knew that the allegations were not true and did its best to put out the facts, but it seemed the damage had already been done. So the school turned to its most powerful weapon in facing the brutal facts—one that is available to every Christian school and that had been employed countless times throughout this process: prayer.

One board member recounts the night of the county commission meeting. "I remember saying to myself that if we get a 7–0 vote I'll know the Lord is with us." It seemed almost impossible. But when the land swap came up on the agenda, it was the opposition leader who made the motion to approve. Then the vote: "All those in favor?" One, two, three, four, five, six, seven. All seven hands went up. Prayer and perseverance had paid off for The King's Academy. Now, years later, the beautiful, 60-acre K-12 campus in West Palm Beach is a testimony to facing the brutal facts with openness, honesty, and God's empowerment.

Addressing the Brutal Facts in the School Context

Christian schools, like other organizations, must face brutal facts on a regular basis. In that a Christian school is more akin to a family than to an industry, even the smallest brutal fact can be critically important to the teacher or to the student who is facing failure, disappointment, or difficulty. More than almost any other enterprise, schools need to maintain an atmosphere of openness and honest debate so that no one's difficulty is overlooked.

In our efforts to run efficient organizations, we cannot ignore the fact that our "products" are the lives we are shaping. We need to realize that our model for handling the difficulties of education and community life will, in many cases, be the lifelong model to which the students will turn.

The principles explored in this book—demonstrating the right kind of leadership, treating people with dignity, facing problems head-on—not only are good ways to run a school but also good principles for conducting our lives. Thus these principles, if the school handles them well, will not only serve the school well but will benefit students for a lifetime. And none of the principles is more true or relevant in life than the principle that calls us to acknowledge and address the brutal facts as opposed to living in denial, which could be considered tantamount to living a lie.

Red-Flag Mechanisms

Yet another concept highlighted by Collins is the need for red-flag mechanisms. His research points out that both the good-to-great companies and their comparison companies had access to virtually the same information. Collins writes, "The key, then, lies not in better information but in turning information into information that cannot be ignored" (page 79). A red-flag mechanism is a mechanism that turns information into "impossible-to-ignore" information.

We saw some of these red-flag systems at work in the previous chapter. One example is the process of teacher evaluation. The curriculum director at many schools is commissioned with knowing what is going on in the classroom and with looking for inconsistencies or breakdowns in the overall curriculum. Teacher evaluation is key to carrying out these responsibilities.

Many schools have worked hard to improve the teacher evaluation process, in part by including evaluations not only from supervisors but from students and peers. Bellevue sets aside seven half days a year for peer collaboration as another way to increase the teachers' use of teamwork and to close curricular gaps.

Two other significant red-flag mechanisms are measuring outputs and putting in place a healthy and transparent appeals policy. The first, measuring outputs, will be touched on in chapter 5. For now, suffice it to say that student and parent surveys are key aspects of this mechanism. They often provide early warning signs of potential problems.

Perhaps the best red-flag mechanism is really not a mechanism at all but more of an attitude or philosophy—"transparent appeals policy." In many organizations the chain of command goes only one way. Thus, "because the boss said so" becomes an adequate explanation and justification for policy and practice. Dissent is perceived as insubordination. The leadership in the Growing Greatness schools, however, welcomed other views and actively courted dissenting feedback.

Bill Safstrom, principal of Bellevue, explained, "If parents don't agree with one of my decisions, they're free to appeal that decision to the superintendent. I don't resent them going up the chain of command. I'm just as interested in getting the decision right as they are." Two things can happen when someone goes up the chain of command with a respected Level 5 leader. Either the decision that has been made will be reaffirmed or it will be reversed because there is a better answer. The right team members will respond positively to either of these results. As Bill puts it, "We don't let decisions destroy relationships."

A sense of teamwork and a focus on mission allows great schools to care more about getting it right than about protecting someone's ego or about winners and losers in power struggles. In fact, this climate must be in place if this emphasis on transparency is to succeed. I surveyed dozens of teachers on this point, and most were able to identify that the head of their school was not only on their side but also cared enough to intervene if a teacher was making the wrong decisions. The reversal of a teacher's decision was viewed not as a rebuke but as a help. The teachers also believed that their head of school would never embarrass them in such a situation and would in fact go out of his or her way to honor the teacher even if a decision was overturned. Such openness, trust, and caring is essential if a school is going to be able to trust and react appropriately to its red-flag mechanisms.

Obviously our Growing Greatness schools were not immune to difficulties. On the contrary, they were on the lookout for them. Using a combination of red-flag mechanisms and the head-on confrontation with the brutal facts our schools were able to build a winning formula for moving from good to great.

CHAPTER 5

The Centrality of Mission to the Christian School

The Hedgehog Concept

The hedgehog concept is probably Collins' most intriguing and colorful good-to-great concept. It originates in a story: A hedgehog and fox are in competition. The fox wants to devour the hedgehog (a fitting metaphor for competition in the business world). The clever, resourceful fox tries daily to devise a new strategy to overcome the hedgehog. The seemingly overmatched hedgehog has only one strategy—however, it's a strategy that the hedgehog is very good at, one that thwarts the fox's attack every time. No matter what form the fox's attack takes, the hedgehog simply rolls into a ball, exposing its sharp quills to its adversary. The fox inevitably returns to its lair with a mouthful of quills.

The lesson is that one does not need to be an expert at everything to succeed. One needs only be the best at something. The hedgehog concept, when applied by a company, organization, or school, is the ability to find the one thing it does best.

Collins goes on to explain that a true hedgehog concept must have three components: first, a service, product, or skill at which one can strive to be the best in the whole world; second, a passion for doing that activity; and third, a way of making money doing that activity. It's easy to see why missing one or two of the components will doom an enterprise to failure (page 90ff).

Let me illustrate this by using an example of my mother's "business" career. My grandfather tried to convince my mother that she would be a great farmer's wife. Yet even if she could have been the greatest farmer's wife in the world, she hated living on the farm! She had no passion for what indeed she may have been very good at. She did have a passion for singing, but there was no economic engine that could sustain an evangelical soloist in the days after World War II. But as she began a writing career, my mother discovered that she was quite good at writing children's Sunday School literature. In fact, she became one of the best in the world. Here she was able to combine her skill as a great children's author with her passion for writing and receive a paycheck at the same time. My mother wrote poems and stories that sold very well. Even a public school teacher I visited in Germany knew all about Winkie Bear, my mother's Sunday School character that sold in the millions. (Unfortunately, my mother hadn't fine-tuned her economic engine, and she was always on salary rather than royalties!)

I think you get the point. Almost any enterprise can be measured by how well it blends one's expertise, passion, and the ability to generate income. Collins built a Venn diagram in *Good to Great* using these three concepts (page 96). In his monograph *Good to Great and the Social Sectors* he modified the "economic engine" circle and replaced it with "resource engine" (Monograph, page 19). I have taken the liberty to further modify the diagram to fit the model demonstrated by great Christian schools.

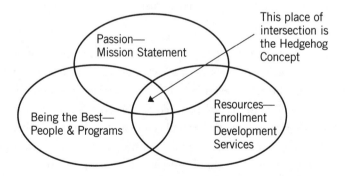

The Christian school's passion must be centered on its mission. Any school can be passionate about great sports teams, state-of-the-art facilities, and improved SAT scores. For the Christian school, however, assets such as these, along with other programs that might lie in the "Being the

Best" category, are always dependent on the right people and must be subservient to the mission.

Finally, the school needs to have the resources to sustain the ministry. Collins actually combines the concept of the economic engine from the business world and the resource engine from the non-profit model in the following grid from his monograph *Good to Great and the Social Sectors* (Monograph, page 21).

Economic Engine in the Social Sectors

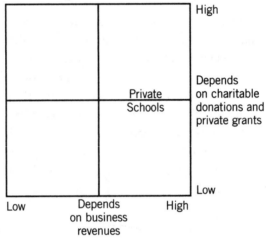

The reason private Christian schools are on the right side of the grid is that, like a business, the school has customers (students and their family) and collects business revenue (tuition). The school must compete for customers and for the disposable income the customers will spend on the school. In this way a private school is much like a business. This, of course, makes the private school quite different from its public school counterpart.

Like a business, a school must learn to maximize its income potential through the development of appropriate programs and use of its facilities. A Christian school, however, like a pure charity, will attract donated dollars only as it produces the outcomes the donors expect. How high the Christian school rises on the vertical axis will depend on the amount of dependence on and success in attracting donations and grants. The success in both attracting customer revenue and charitable giving directly correlates to the school's measurable success in harnessing its passion and achieving its goal of being the best it can be in its chosen areas of focus.

Let's take a look at what this adapted hedgehog model looks like in the great Christian school.

Passion—the Clear Statement of Mission

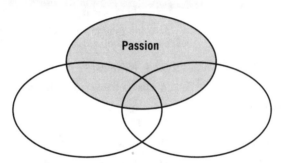

In the schools we studied, the strongest of the three circles seemed to be the passion for the school's mission. Most of the schools were able to condense their mission into a short statement or paragraph; most of the key individuals knew its content, and many could quote it from memory.

Comprehensively studied schools	Vision/Purpose/Mission Statement
Annapolis Area Christian School Severn, Maryland	Our school, in partnership with Christian parents, engages students in a rigorous program of learning from a biblical worldview to serve Jesus Christ faithfully in the world.
Bellevue Christian High School Clyde Hill, Washington	Our mission is to prepare young people to live fully for God in a rapidly changing world with the ability to understand, evaluate, and transform their world from the foundation of God's unchanging values.

Comprehensively studied schools	Vision/Purpose/Mission Statement
Cincinnati Hills Christian Academy Cincinnati, Ohio	Cincinnati Hills Christian Academy is a Christ-centered, nondenominational college preparatory school. Students are educated, encouraged and prepared to grow in a personal faith in Jesus Christ, to pursue higher education, and to serve: the Lord, their families and their communities.
First Presbyterian Day School Macon, Georgia	Our purpose is to educate and equip students to change the world for God's glory.
The King's Academy West Palm Beach, FL	The King's Academy is a Christ-centered college preparatory middle and senior high school for students who have teachable hearts, moldable minds, and coachable spirits. We offer a loving family environment where students are encouraged to grow in their relationships with Jesus, their families, teachers, and others, as they are prepared to be tomorrow's leaders wherever God calls them to serve. We are committed to developing God's best for each student spiritually, academically, morally, and socially through every program and activity.
Westminster Christian Academy St. Louis, Missouri	Westminster Christian Academy honors Jesus Christ by providing an excellent education, rooted in biblical truth as interpreted by the Westminster Confession of Faith, for the children of Christian parents. Faculty and staff enable students to discover (continued)

Comprehensively studied schools	Vision/Purpose/Mission Statement
Westminster Christian Academy St. Louis, Missouri	(continued) and embrace a biblical view of the world and integrate that view into every area of life.
Wheaton Academy West Chicago, Illinois	To nurture growth in our students through relationships, excellence and service to the glory of God.

Wheaton Academy's vision guided the change we read about in chapter 3. Westminster's theologically driven statement has anchored the school in its Reformed tradition and understanding, which has in turn driven the other two circles. First Presbyterian's mission has driven it to attempt to be "the best." Cincinnati Hills' and Bellevue's statements have caused them to measure their schools' outcomes and results.

One of my most interesting experiences of observing a mission statement drive a school's development came during a teacher interview at Wheaton Academy. I asked to a veteran teacher to identify the best things about Wheaton Academy.

"Excellence," the teacher responded. "This school's not afraid to push for excellence—in its athletic program and in student missions. That's why we look for the best coaches and teachers. Second, there are relationships. Our school is the perfect size—not too big, not too small—so that every student can get involved in something." He went on to enumerate a long list of possible student involvements from AP classes to the rock-climbing club. "It's not one-size-fits-all," he said, "so we have a large number of activities, and half of our teachers know the names of every student in the school.

"Finally, there's an emphasis on service. We have built a culture of service. It used to be student-driven, but now it's school-driven. Kids are really thinking more about others and less about themselves."

I was amazed! This teacher really knew the mission statement of Wheaton Academy. He'd just given me dynamic illustrations of its three main points of excellence, relationships, and service as he summarized what Wheaton Academy was all about. In order to tie a bow on our interview and let him know that he had just given me the school's purpose statement as the answer to my question, I asked rhetorically, "And what is Wheaton Academy's mission statement?"

I did not receive the answer I expected. He hesitated, then looked embarrassed, and finally sheepishly explained, "I guess I should know that." It was both obvious and refreshing that he hadn't given me a canned description of the school based on what its mission statement said it should be. He had given me a spontaneous and genuine description of what Wheaton Academy had actually become in the past fifteen years.

Still pondering his answer, I began another teacher interview, this one with a second-year teacher who began our interview by quoting the purpose statement verbatim. I confided that the teacher I'd interviewed previously could describe the school in terms of the purpose statement but couldn't recite the statement itself. The new teacher explained, "The teachers here may not be able to recite the purpose statement because they *are* the purpose statement. Wheaton Academy *hires* the purpose statement." That is, it hires teachers who reflect and value excellence, relationships, and service, all to God's glory. As one who had a hand in the original crafting of the mission statement over fifteen years ago, I was gratified to find that it has become a core descriptor for what the school is, not merely what the school would like to be.

All of the Growing Greatness schools we studied had mission statements that were both quoted and illustrated. One school listed in the best practices section of this book, Lutheran High School North of Macomb, Michigan, began every faculty meeting by reading its purpose statement. The principal, Steve Buuck, told me the following story that illustrated just how important that mission statement had become as a reminder of why the teachers were there. Steve was prepared to begin the faculty meeting following the death of one of their teachers from an aggressive cancer. As he struggled to begin this emotional meeting, one of the teachers stopped him. "Dr. Buuck, can we start the meeting by reading the mission statement?" He recited, "Within our rich Christian tradition, Lutheran High School North is devoted to academic excellence and, above all, to sharing and modeling the Gospel of Jesus Christ in all aspects of its ministry by providing students diverse opportunities to serve their Savior while serving others." These teachers needed to be reminded of why they were there, and they received the comfort that a colleague had spent her working life making a difference, responding to a call, and accomplishing a mission.

Being the Best—People and Programs

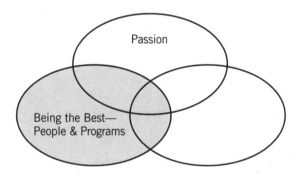

Each of the schools had produced a desire for excellence that grew out of the mission. Gregg Thompson of First Presbyterian emphasized that being a thoroughly Christian school requires doing one's best and seeking excellence. It seemed that each school had identified programs, projects, and practices that would reflect excellence and that had the potential to put the school in the category of "the best" in a particular dimension.

One school actually began by asking Collins' question, "What could we be the best at?" and then wrote the mission statement! Unfortunately, this school was too small to be included in our study; however, after having conversations with other school heads who had participated in our study, Ron Polinder, Head of the Rehoboth Christian School, gave me a call.

Ron was in charge of running a daylong seminar at the upcoming CSI

(Christian Schools International) convention incorporating Jim Collins' good-to-great principles. He called to see if I could help. Several meaningful conversations ensued. The most helpful for our purposes was Ron's explanation of Rehoboth Christian School's use of the hedgehog concept. Ron had been working through *Good to Great* with his administrative staff. When they arrived at the chapter on the hedgehog principle, they asked themselves, "What could we be the best at, if not in the whole world, at least in our part of the world?"

This exercise resulted in three primary areas in which Rehoboth believed it could excel: academics, diversity, and Christian perspective. The three primary areas became the basis for the school's new tagline: "Vigorously Academic, Beautifully Diverse, Thoroughly Christian." Having identified what it could be the best at, the school could now focus on these identified areas for excellence with the sustained passion and resources needed to drive its hedgehog concept.

Resources—Money Management

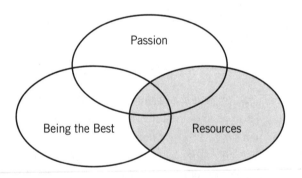

Our Growing Greatness schools all do a good job balancing their budgets. Tuition provides the lion's share of the Christian school's revenue, and all the schools separated their operating budgets from their large capital campaign budgets. How they each provided their scholarship dollars, however, differed.

Some schools charged their full-paying students up to 5 percent over cost in order to provide a pool for scholarships. The rationale is that a socioeconomically diverse campus is a benefit for all students and that the full-paying student is paying for this benefit. Other schools simply went out and raised up to 10 percent of their operating budget for scholarships.

The schools demonstrated a priority of recruiting the right students for their mission. One example of a model recruiting program is found in chapter 11. The story of Cindy Sielana at Catholic Central highlights what getting the right person in the right seat can mean for a school's recruitment program. Schools reported that as they flourished in achieving their "passion" and being "the best," the right students seemed to follow.

The second primary source of resources for the Christian school is charitable giving. I will touch on this topic only briefly, since there are many excellent professional groups that are willing to help a school build a professional approach to fundraising and financial development. One such group is PAIDEIA, Inc., led by Dr. Bruce Lockerbie. His excellent manual, *From Candy Sales to Committed Donors*, does an outstanding job of deciphering both the "why" and the "how-to" of a strong financial development program for the Christian school. One of the Growing Greatness schools could have been a "poster school" for this transformation.

"We were the number one seller of Sally Foster wrapping paper in the U.S.," said Gregg Thompson, headmaster of First Presbyterian Day School. "We spent our entire development energy on the annual wrapping paper sale with the upside being $100,000 in sales with $50,000 going to the school. With help from PAIDEIA, Inc. we cancelled our wrapping paper sales and moved to a disciplined and professional approach to financial development. We are presently completing a 7 million dollar campaign to add a new secondary classroom building." The transformation is a testimony to the fruits of working hard and working smart, and the soon-to-be-finished secondary school building proves that the school is the obvious winner.

The third leg of the resource stool is the revenue that can be gained from extending services. Many schools offer extended services (summer school, camps, sports, music, drama, academics, etc.), which makes use of an otherwise empty facility. Up until now these have brought in only marginal income, although they have helped supplement teachers' and coaches' salaries. Now, however, schools are beginning to build for the multiple uses of their facilities both in the summer and during the school year. This development has been spurred by a sense of stewardship in desiring to share the school's facilities with the larger church family as well as to increase services income.

An example of this deliberate plan to be both a good steward of its facilities and build a revenue stream is Annapolis. The leadership of Annapolis Christian formulated a philosophy for the use of their campus and has begun to plan and build with that philosophy in mind. An area church now worships in the school's new auditorium. The school is planning to rent its new indoor lacrosse field to premier clubs and teams. Larry Kooi, superintendent of Annapolis, explains that donors have been very positive, realizing that the school is using its new facilities to their full advantage both for expanded ministry and for revenue.

Another particular example of the win-win possibilities of working with other Christian groups is the partnership between Wheaton Academy and Willow Creek Community Church. Willow Creek Wheaton is currently worshiping in the Wheaton Academy's new Fine Arts Center. Having spent over four million dollars on this facility, the Academy was short on resources to outfit the new auditorium. The solution? Willow Creek installed the required sound, light, and video capabilities, state-of-the-art media that it needed for its satellite hook-up with its main campus.

Putting It All Together
While the first three concepts we've looked at—Level 5 Leadership; First Who, Then What; and Confronting the Brutal Facts—all seem to be essential ingredients in great schools, it's the hedgehog concept that puts them all together. A continual focus on the overlap of passion, excellence, and revenue management has proved to be a formula for success in the Growing Greatness schools studied.

Conversations with school leaders, faculty, staff, and constituents made it clear, however, that not all three factors of the hedgehog are equal. The passion or mission drives everything else. This was in part why Annapolis Christian came up with a philosophy of facilities use prior to allowing others to use its campus. No amount of money or success in a particular sport or activity should drive a school away from its mission. The beauty of the hedgehog principle is that it is the intersection of all three components—the mission never moves. The mission serves as the anchor as a school chooses from the possibilities of what it could be best at. The mission determines under what circumstances and at what cost revenues will be sought. This of course highlights the need for a clear and well-articulated mission. (See the chart earlier in this chapter.)

Many colleges and elite prep schools have drifted from their founding mission as a result of chasing programs and revenue. Perhaps you can point to countless examples of this tragedy. In his recent book *Conceiving the Christian College*, Duane Litfin, president of Wheaton College, outlines how this loss of mission has taken place in American schools. He also points out that this drift can be checked only by resolute leadership at the board and administrative level in maintaining a school's Christian mission. Indeed, this commitment and discipline was evident in all of our Growing Greatness schools.

CHAPTER 6

Accelerators of Success

Technology and other Accelerators

Collins discussed one accelerator of success, namely technology, in his book *Good to Great*. This chapter will highlight technology along with three other factors that function as accelerators to success. But first a word about a perceived major contributor to success that is typically overrated: technology. Collins warns (page 154) against the "technology trap" of thinking that technology will create rather than sustain momentum. The accuracy of this observation was borne out in all of the schools we studied. No matter how technologically advanced the school, no one identified technology as a driver, or even as a key component, of its success.

Bellevue Christian High School, for example, is situated in the home-town of Microsoft. It has "smart" classrooms and technology that would be the envy of most Christian schools. But even here technology is treated merely as an enabler. "It's how you use it that counts," says principal Bill Safstrom. He recognizes that without a master teacher in the class-room even the best available technology would be of little use.

Is technology then unimportant? On the contrary, the teachers themselves found great value in the use of technology. It not only helped them to be more effective in their teaching, but it affirmed their school's commitment to them as professionals.

While teachers universally bemoan limited funding that seems to contain Christian school salaries well below their public school counterparts, the teachers from our Growing Greatness schools felt valued and appreciated when provided with proper technology. In fact, providing appropriate technology may arguably be among the most cost-effective ways to increase teacher effectiveness and satisfaction, which, as Collins describes, would make it an accelerator of the school's success.

The following three factors that will be highlighted here function as accelerators to success. But unlike technology, they also have some potential to drive success. These factors are curriculum development, college guidance, and parent involvement.

Curriculum Development

Many of the schools studied had a full-time curriculum development specialist on staff. You may remember Barry Shealy at First Presbyterian Day School from chapter 2. "He drives us crazy," confessed one teacher. But she acknowledged that he had raised standards and integrated the curriculum to be not only academically sound but also to reflect a Christian worldview in every discipline. One result is that the school has become a National Blue Ribbon School recognized by the U.S. Department of Education.

The person with the role of providing direction for the curriculum more often than not was also responsible for training and implementing the school's philosophy and overall Christian worldview (see Evangelical Christian School, chapter 9). Having someone with this distinct responsibility has had a tremendously positive impact on the schools studied.

College Guidance

The second accelerator to success relates to college advisement. Parents especially confirmed the importance of a good program of college advisement. This should come as no surprise, given that these days some parents will spend thousands of dollars for a college admissions coach, test preparation, and college visits. Because the final step in nurturing students is to ensure that their next step will be to a place where they will continue to develop, providing services in the area of college advisement can be a win-win situation for the school as it meets a need of parents and students alike.

In many cases the value assigned to the role of college and career counseling reflected the strength of the person in that role. Wheaton

Academy hired the former director of admissions from Wheaton College, someone who served as president of the Christian College Consortium Association of Admission Directors. Annapolis Christian hired Mary Sue Burgess, a former analyst at Gulf Oil with an MBA.

I visited with Mary Sue. "Pick a card, any card, and then read it out loud," she said. I selected a 3x5 card from the deck fanned out in front of me and read, "Jeremiah 1:5a—Before I formed you in the womb I knew you, before you were born I set you apart."

"Pick another card." I reach for the white lined 3x5 cards and read, "Psalm 121:8—The Lord will watch over your coming and going both now and forevermore." Mary Sue explained, "This is how I begin every interview with students. I want them to know God has a plan for their life and that finding the right college will be part of that plan. That plan may even be the opposite of what the student is thinking when he or she first meets with me.

"We begin with prayer. Then I ask what the student and his or her parents are thinking. And then I introduce them to the tools they can use."

These tools include the Parent Recommendation Form, which allows her to get in touch with the parents' thinking, and the "My Take on Me" sheet, which allows the students to reflect as they fill in four pages of questions about themselves, their calling, giftedness, experiences, qualifications, and more. She also has the students fill out a "Brag Sheet" so that she can highlight their strengths with potential admissions counselors. And then I was handed an annotated list of 27 websites that could help the student with his or her search. The goal of all this work is for the student to build a grid of potential colleges from distinctly Christian to secular, from safe bet to real stretch. Mary Sue works through all the options with students and their families.

"I find that nearly 50 percent of the parents get actively involved with me in the student's search. This guidance seems to be really valued by our school's families." Mary Sue relayed some of the stories of how God has guided her students. "I'm getting chills," she admitted as she recounted a particularly miraculous story of a student getting into her dream college. Mary Sue's genuine love for the kids and the level of calling she feels as she attempts to guide them came through in a powerful way. I can't imagine a parent not appreciating this bonus dimension to an Annapolis Christian education.

The value added by a quality college counseling program seemed to be the norm for our Growing Greatness schools. This function, somewhat administrative in nature, can become a powerful accelerator in the hands of the right person and administration.

Expecting More from Parents and Getting It

Perhaps the greatest accelerator of all, however, is healthy, positive parent involvement. This flies in the face of what some perceive as the public school mentality: "Keep the parents out of the schools and leave the teaching to the professionals." This mentality is too often echoed by the Christian schools. One of our Growing Greatness administrators had to admit, "Parental involvement has not always been the case in Christian schools and specifically at our school. In fact, the traditional model held that 'we know what we're doing and how we want to do it. If you do not like it, you are free to leave.' Parental opinions and ideas were treated with distrust and certainly not solicited." But that was years ago, and now parents are vibrantly involved in the school.

The King's Academy exemplifies a campus that models positive parental involvement. It fact, it has made a conscious decision to take advantage of such involvement. One parent explained it this way: "Because the administration has demonstrated confidence in the parents, the parents have stepped up and are able to promote many of the successful programs of the school."

At The King's Academy, the K–12 campus now has 200 parents involved on campus each week. "The school is open to parent talent," explained one parent. "You need that talent in order to get the school to where it needs to go." In addition to the parent organizations, committees, and volunteer opportunities, King's has made a concerted effort to garner parents' prayer support. One of the unusual features of the academy's new campus is its dedicated prayer room, which was built so that parents could come and pray for their students and the school.

As I was interviewing a group of parents, one mother explained that she was a "Monday Mom." Another identified herself as a "Wednesday Mom." These were the days on which they were committed to come to the school and pray.

Every campus I visited had enthusiastic, involved parents telling success stories about their school. This parent involvement not only helps with the work of the school but also elicits scores of enthusiastic boosters for the school in the larger community.

By now, you may have noticed the use of the words positive or constructive attached to parent involvement. Obviously not all parental involvement is positive or constructive. The leaders of all of our Growing Greatness school recognized the need for managing parent involvement. But all share Randy Brunk's analysis: "Sure, it takes time to manage parent involvement, but the payoff is well worth it. My parents are a big reason for our success at Cincinnati Hills Christian Academy."

In fact, technology, curriculum development, college guidance, and parent involvement all seem to be accelerators of success as long as they are rightly managed by strong Level 5 leaders.

CHAPTER 7

The Power of Doing the Right Things the Right Way Over Time

The Flywheel

I n his closing chapters Collins points out that a culture of disciplined application of the good-to-great principles will lead to a cycle of continuous improvement and accomplishment. Collins depicts this as the process of pushing a giant flywheel into motion. While it takes extraordinary effort to get the flywheel moving that first inch, the same principle of inertia will make it virtually unstoppable once it's rolling.

In the schools included in this study, some processes that required monumental effort at the outset, once in place, seemed to create monumental positive results. Furthermore, these positive results produced unanticipated benefits.

Building Momentum

It was gratifying to see the unintended fruit of a school's best practices, especially when the school had worked so hard to make the changes. Nowhere was this truer than in the area of student discipline. Several schools set out to deliberately move student discipline from law to grace (see the story of Lutheran North in chapter 12), from rules to responsibility (Wheaton Academy), and from demerits to relationships (The King's Academy).

Wheaton Academy's transformation has led to what principal Jon Keith described as students "policing themselves." He describes how a few years earlier a group of senior students had presented a petition that the dress code be changed to require girls to wear longer skirts. These students believed that the present standard didn't reflect biblical standards; they wanted to help teach other students, especially the underclassmen, the importance of dressing modestly and not creating a problem for young men. Talk about turning things around.

Years ago when I was a teacher in Christian school, I remember a transfer student from the local public school stopping me after class, "What gives here?" he asked. "At my old school it wasn't cool to study. My friends and I used to go out at night and see what kind of trouble we could get into. Here everybody studies; in fact, you're not cool unless you do study!" My student friend was experiencing the power of positive peer pressure.

At Annapolis Area Christian School a student prefect board now handles most cases of discipline involving the student honor code. David Castle, principal at AACS, told me that often the students will ask just to be punished rather than have to go before the student prefect board, not because the prefect board members are unfair or harsh but because peer pressure is so powerful. These and other Christian schools are learning to harness the power of positive peer pressure.

Recently an AACS freshman was brought before a prefect committee hearing for "borrowing" too much of other people's work to complete his freshman essay. The prefect board required him to show up at school on a Saturday morning to learn how to write and cite his own work and sources. Who showed up that Saturday morning to help this struggling freshman student? The prefect who had handed down the punishment. What a picture of Christ, who judging our sin as Righteous King then bends down to reconcile us back as Suffering Savior. The beauty of this process is that students are growing and the situation didn't require a meeting with the vice-principal.

One of the most dramatic discipline transitions was at The King's Academy, which had a long tradition of discipline by demerits. Demerits were handed out in all twelve grades, and any student who had accumulated a certain number within a week would be called into the office for a detention. I had experienced a similar disciplinary scheme in the Christian grade school I attended in the 1960s.

What once had been culturally appropriate and cutting edge (it was called "behavior modification") had degenerated into a game at The King's Academy. Students would try to get just enough demerits each week without breaking the threshold to get into "real" trouble. What was intended to protect the student-teacher relationship by having an impartial discipline meted out by the school office was now preventing students and teachers from building relationships and dealing with issues. Things had to change.

The genius of The King's Academy transformation was that they didn't just eliminate what wasn't working; they brought in a new strategy—The Flip Flippen strategy for classroom discipline. The Flippen Group has formalized a training program based on its founder's research and teaching called "Capturing Kids' Hearts." This program is designed to train teachers to manage classroom discipline around innovative teaching techniques—including social contracts and mutual respect. The campus has also implemented a prefect system that enables the students to exercise leadership and responsibility.

Like pushing on a giant flywheel, this transformation was very difficult at first. Several teachers and even administrators protested the new system. But with consistent leadership at the top and continued pressure on the flywheel, the campus has been dramatically changed. Teacher Mrs. Trisha Reelitz described the transformation: "I truly dreaded the switch from the Tally System of discipline to a more relational approach. Having taught for sixteen years using that yellow 3x5 card as my only tangible method of discipline, I felt extremely inadequate to handle discipline in a new way. What I soon realized early on in the 'no tallies' shift was that student resentment had grown in the past from our allowing them to err up to ten times without consequence, then slamming them with a consequence on the eleventh infraction. The battle lines had been drawn, and the fight continued between us and them. At about the same time as the shift began, I attended a workshop touting the value of building strong relationships with students to garner their respect and trust. Shaking my students' hands on a daily basis coupled with a more relaxed atmosphere in the classroom freed me to use creative methods of discipline. I now feel extremely free to demonstrate my appreciation and love for my students, building caring relationships while truly getting to know their concerns. The proof of the value of a more relational approach to discipline is students who make an effort to speak to their teachers as they walk through the halls—quite a difference from those resentful students under the tally system who avoided eye-contact and conversation."

This new discipline system not only gave teachers a better way to do discipline but has helped "move the school from adult centered to student centered," as Tony Miner, Dean of The King's Academy, described it. This new atmosphere and focus has become a large flywheel helping to move The King's Academy from good to great.

Expecting More—Student Energy as an Accelerator

"We try to assume that our students are two years older in maturity in their chronological age rather than two years younger. We find that most of the time students rise to your expectations," explains Jon Keith of Wheaton Academy. This certainly seemed to be the case when Chip Huber launched his Project L.E.A.D. program several years ago. The goal was to encourage senior class leadership by having a group of students go through leadership training the summer before their senior year. They would experience authentic community and mentoring relationships.

As Chip's seniors did show strong and extraordinary leadership during the following school year, Chip continued to give these groups larger and larger visions of leadership, not just for the school but for the world. Well, the students stepped up beyond Chip's wildest expectations.

"The group of eleven seniors I was working with that summer," Chip explained, "was exposed to a program called 'One Life Revolution,' co-sponsored by World Vision and Youth Specialties. It was organized to help high school students respond in a practical way to the AIDS pandemic that was ravaging sub-Saharan Africa. This particular program challenged students to raise money for the practical needs of orphans in Zambia. I was expecting the students to respond by increasing campus awareness of the need and organizing a reasonable fundraising effort to purchase some appropriate practical items such as a well, a garden, sponsoring some orphans, and other things like these. The students, after prayer and discussion, felt God directing us to build a school for a community of children who had never had the chance to be educated—a school that would cost over $50,000. The student passion and conviction was so genuine that I said that I would approach the administration.

"Fundraising in Christian school environments can be very competitive and I wasn't exactly sure how the administration would respond. However, after prayer, discussion and agreement that this could be organized in such a way as to reinforce the school's mission and would require the students doing the work (i.e., not merely asking Mom and Dad for donations and giving from their own resources), it was approved.

"I still wasn't sure that we hadn't bitten off more than we could chew. However, in the weeks and months ahead I was amazed by the students' leadership, creativity, and focus in reaching their goals. Not only did we build a school with the $78,000 we raised that first year, but in the last three years we have raised an additional $325,000 which has been used to build a health clinic, provide long-term security, food, AIDS education training, homes for orphan-headed household, a center for child evangelism ministry work, and many other community development needs.

"The Zambia Project has been life changing for both our student community at Wheaton Academy and for thousands of children at great risk with incredible needs on the other side of the globe. Our students have both learned and proven that when they are given real opportunity to chase the dream God has for their lives, they can and will literally change the world."

In addition to exposing its students to the needs of others, Wheaton Academy's Zambia Project has created a "culture of service" on the campus. Students, faculty, and administration highlighted this culture throughout the interviews. Service, as you may recall from chapter 4, was one of Wheaton Academy's mission goals. Allowing students to provide leadership and energy accelerated the achievement of the school's goal.

A similar acceleration came to The King's Academy on January 23, 2006. This date had been mentioned several times early in my campus visit as a transformational day in the school's life, but I hadn't heard the story until I met with Gary Butler, the chaplain and a Bible teacher. He explained that the school had started a chapel leadership class with the educational goal of teaching leadership within a Christian context and the practical job of planning most of the chapel services.

The End of the Spear had just been released, and the class had planned to relate a chapel service to that movie. During the planning, however, one of the students spoke: "I don't think this is what we need right now; first, we need to deal with the sin in our lives." The other students agreed but they couldn't decide how to organize a chapel around that theme. Finally, they decided that they would spend that weekend praying and bring back what they believed the Lord would have them say in chapel on Monday.

Monday arrived, and Gary started the chapel by explaining what the chapel class had been thinking and praying about regarding sin in one's life. Then Gary panicked a few teachers by announcing that the rest of the chapel would be an open microphone event. For the next hour students came out of their seats to confess their sins, ask for forgiveness, and challenge their fellow students to live for Christ. "It was the most unbelievable chapel I've ever been a part of, all because we trusted the students enough to let them take the lead. In the wake of that chapel, revival broke out; Bible studies broke out; prayer times broke out." Gary then read me a prayer written by one of the students from the chapel class, which read in part:

> I pray that as we walk out of here this morning, that we will open our eyes and our ears to Your voice and direct our focus on You. That we will not leave this gym just like an ordinary chapel to just fall back into our regular routine of life, forgetting what we heard.
> ...I desperately pray that as this new semester begins that we will begin to, as a school, represent You, the King of Kings, like You so justly deserve. ...In Jesus' Name I pray. Amen.

Service—the Untapped Tool of Learning

Many of the schools studied had a formal Christian service component to their curriculum. Two of the most successful models were Westminster and Cincinnati Hills.

The Cincinnati Hills program is called S.O.S. (Student Organized Service). Karen Hordinski, the Student Service Coordinator, explained that the name came from the first group of student volunteers. "The philosophy is that kids grow by doing service," said Karen. "That's why we try to have them do as much of the organizational work as possible. They even came up with the name. The kids really run the program. We've tried to organize around what the students are passionate about. And we're not just talking about being 'do-gooders' or Band-Aid people. These students really get involved at a significant level and make a difference."

The kids have organized into over twenty S.O.S. groups. The groups largely work with established non-profit organizations such as Habitat for Humanity, elementary schools, and local level charities. The students have also taken initiative to launch their own programs. One student wrote a grant and received local funding to transport Cincinnati Hills students to and from tutoring assignments.

In addition to these service teams, S.O.S. organizes quarterly service days where any student can pitch in. Mission trips are also organized during breaks in the school and their January, or "J," term. Karen explains that the school doesn't want to compete with church sponsored summer mission trips. This guideline and an attempt to stay away from fundraising are the only two restrictions that the S.O.S. program places upon itself.

The program is energized by the school's requirement that each student accumulate 120 hours of service during his or her four years of high school at Cincinnati Hills. Thirty hours are required each year; half of those hours are spent serving people in need, and two mission experiences are required. These requirements are aimed at broadening the students' exposure to the world's physical and spiritual needs.

"As a Christian school we are sheltered from many of the harmful things we might face, but we're not secluded. Through S.O.S. and mission trips we're presented with the world and we're ready for it," said one student leader.

I asked Karen about the logistics of implementing such a program. First, she pointed to the fact that the considerable administrative burden of tracking the students' required hours of service was handled by the school's central office. Second, the students do much of the work. Karen has organized training days for student leaders (open to anyone) so that she can properly prepare student leaders. Finally, she points to the support of parents who, along with faculty members, staff the mission trips, supply transportation and generally help out.

Karen explains that there are always a few seniors struggling to get all their hours in before graduation. But she says that generally things are moving smoothly and students are "getting to see the world through the eyes of God."

Similarly, Westminster's Senior Service Program is built into the curriculum. Only seniors are required to participate. The program takes place each Thursday morning; Westminster's modified block schedule makes it possible to schedule this morning of service.

During junior year each student selects a Senior Service Project. Most students, like at Cincinnati Hills, work through existing agencies. And like at Cincinnati Hills, many students have been profoundly affected. One year a senior girl worked in a home for abandoned children. Her whole family became involved in the mission even to the point of adopting one of the children.

Former students from both Westminster and Cincinnati Hills are on the mission field today because of their involvement in missions during their high school years. Here we see the flywheel effect beyond graduation—in fact, we see its effect for eternity.

BEST PRACTICES

*The story of best practices demonstrated by a variety
of great Christian secondary schools.*

*While time limited the number of schools that could participate in
the comprehensive study, many best practices were identified in a broad
spectrum of Christian schools. The five schools selected are very diverse:
one Lutheran, two Christian Schools International (CSI) schools, two
Catholic schools, and one Association of Christian Schools
International (ACSI) school.*

*One goal in selecting such diverse schools was to encourage schools to
look for best practices wherever they might find them. Too often we look
only to similar schools or organizations for lessons to learn, ignoring the
whole world outside our smaller subcultures and traditions. Recognizing
that all truth is God's truth, we should be bold in looking for it wherever
we might find it. Many of the schools in this study regularly visit public
schools as well as elite secular prep schools to see what they can learn.*

*The even more fundamental reason these schools were selected is
because they are excellent examples of best practices leading to greatness
in providing Christian secondary education. I hope you enjoy reading
these stories as much as I had in seeing them at work.*

CHAPTER 8

A Class Sister Act

The Story of Level 5 Leadership

Sister Joan glanced over my shoulder and out the open door of her office. Realizing that the receptionist had stepped away she excused herself and picked up the phone before it could go to voicemail. "Hello ... How is she doing? ... When will she be able to have visitors? ... Well, I'll be down there just as soon as she feels up to it ... You are so welcome ... Goodbye, and God bless you." By not allowing the phone to go to voicemail, recognizing the voice on the other end, listening compassionately and communicating that she cared, Sister Joan was demonstrating what I had heard about her all day.

After a full day on the campus of Xavier College Preparatory in Phoenix, Arizona, I realized that I had witnessed a Level 5 leader at work. All day I had heard about communication ("Sister Joan's door is always open," "You can talk to her about anything," "She always listens,"), community ("She treats all 1,150 students like they're her kids," "The parents are always welcome to be on campus and be involved," "Sister Joan was there for me when things were tough"), and consistency ("You may not always like the discipline but you know it's fair," "Doesn't have any favorites," "Everyone is treated the same," "You know she cares and she is always fair").

Communication, community, and consistency describe Xavier Prep. They reflect the thirty-two year leadership of Sister Joan Fitzgerald. Her quiet and disarming manner had put me at ease when I had met her early in the day. When I inquired about her school's success she pointed me to an elaborate board structure that had two full boards and five active committees with forty-seven members in all. She praised her administrative team and teachers for developing great programs and making a difference for kids. Several times she highlighted a special program such as the "Great Books" curriculum or the fine arts department. Each story would start out with "the teacher that made it happen." Sister Joan also talked about the critical involvement of the parents. "We wouldn't have anything without our parents," she declared.

Sister Joan's leadership style was so genuine and natural that I almost missed the key factor: In classic Level 5 leadership style she was giving away all the credit. Let's take a closer look at Sister Joan's Level 5 leadership and how her best practices of communication, community, and consistency have shaped Xavier Prep.

Communication

"Her door is always open." That open door seemed to be a trademark of Sister Joan. I finally asked some of the staff if this is something that Sister Joan says often. (I have personally worked for several bosses who *said* their door was always open but with a tone of voice and demeanor that also said, "I'd rather you never walk through it!") No one could ever remember Sister Joan actually saying or writing the words, "My door is always open" or that "I have an open door policy" anywhere. It was simply true; her door was always open. I knew that her invitation was genuine because I experienced it. Obviously her faculty and staff had also experienced it.

Even the students noticed this ability to listen. One told me that "when you talk to her [Sister Joan] you know she genuinely cares. She told me what activities she thought would be good for me. I was shocked that she would take that time for me when there are 1,200 others!" Another student explained, "Sister Joan treats us like family."

But how does one operate a multimillion dollar enterprise with hundreds of customers and thousands of constituents with her door open to all? The answer is found in the second theme that reflects Sister Joan's leadership—community.

Community

While "community" was the number one descriptor I heard throughout my visit, it reflected more than simply feeling at home. It described an elaborate matrix of board, administrator, teacher, parent, and student organizations that created the community. And this community has one primary purpose—that each of Xavier Prep's students will succeed.

Xavier lives out the understanding of I Corinthians, which teaches that every member of the body has a part to play. All students are encouraged to succeed not only in their curricular work but in their extracurricular activities as well, where their God-given talents and interests can be developed.

The Vice Principal of Activities and Athletic Director, Sister Lynn Winsor, challenges students each year with these words: "If you're not involved in an extracurricular activity, come and see me and we'll find one for you." Almost all students graduate with multiple clubs, activities, and recognitions behind their names.

Students spoke proudly about the many activities in which they were involved. They told of peers who were uninterested in school until they became leaders in a newly started club or activity. "Every girl here has her own thing and that's what makes us proud of each other," explained one student. The list of possible activities seems almost endless, but the goal is the same—that each girl will have multiple success experiences as she grows and exercises her God-given talents.

The high correlation with future success makes these extracurricular involvements key to achieving the school's mission statement goal: "Xavier College Preparatory is a Catholic community that strives to prepare young women with the knowledge, skills, and integrity to meet the challenges of a changing global society in a positive and productive manner. This pursuit of excellence, individual and cooperative, is our mission."

In order to create this level of opportunity for students, the school has to be mobilized into effective teams that are empowered to act. This requires elaborate involvement on behalf of the administration, teachers, and parents.

Earlier I mentioned that 47 adults were mobilized at the board level. At first I thought that this meant that the board was merely a fundraising tool where people paid to have their names on the list. I found, however, that an executive group the size of a typical school board handled the traditional governance issues while other board committees tackled more specialized areas. The standing committees are strategic planning, communication and advocacy, facilities, development, and technology. A separate foundation board and an advisory board include the involvement of several parent groups. The goal of these boards is building an endowment for the school and purchasing needed adjacent properties.

Each of these boards and board committees has been delegated a great deal of autonomy, and each works hard to achieve its goals. The boards and committees are self-perpetuating for continuity and momentum as they tackle their respective objectives. The result of this structure is not only a great deal of ownership and achievement but also communication. With this many people close to the senior level of leadership, a great deal of information is being passed on. Currently, however, the Board of Trustees is not happy with the existing level of communication and has made it a strategic goal to "expand the existing communications plan to strengthen the sense of community among all Xavier constituencies with regular reinforcement of the community's shared values, and enhance the communications that keep all constituents well informed about school matters, as well as more effectively communicate the Xavier story to the greater Phoenix metropolitan area."

The community is being built not only at the school's lay leadership level but also through the active parent organization. Instead of having a typical parent organization, Xavier Preparatory has two very different organizations: the Mothers' Guild and the Dads' Club. Both have a devoted following, sponsor special activities for the parents as well as the students, and are active in supporting the school. The club nature of the groups makes for some wonderful camaraderie and a real energy for each club's activities. There are very few men only and women only organizations in our culture; these two organizations seem to take advantage of this unique experience for adults to work together for a common good.

Some may ask, "How does this community structure make it possible for Sister Joan to keep her door open? I would think having all these organizations and parents involved would only make it worse." The secret to keeping each of these groups as well as the students on task is the third leg of Sister Joan's leadership: consistency.

Consistency

Earlier in this book we talked about the flywheel and how long it sometimes takes to get the flywheel rolling. Well, after thirty-two years of leadership Sister Joan has the flywheel rolling with clearly defined roles and repeatable systems.

This consistency can be seen in everything, beginning with the school's discipline code and its consistent enforcement. "If you're consistent you don't have to backtrack. Whether the student likes it or not, they know it's the same for everybody," said Sister Joan. This consistency is echoed by the administrative staff. "The expectations are clearly communicated and we have the students sign the guidelines each year to indicate they understand and will follow them," said Sister Lynn.

But how do the students feel about this consistency when it comes to discipline? "They have strict rules here, but I'd rather have that than the alternative," explains one student. "I need the discipline; if I don't have structure I won't follow through," said another. I heard the word fair a lot. The phrase, "you may not like it but it's *fair*," explained consistently enforced rules, whether related to the school's dress code or the attendance policy. This concept of fairness seemed to be the governor that kept discipline from sliding into legalism and the "rules for rules' sake" that plagues so many Christian schools.

Consistency was also seen in the level of detail in processes and procedures. This was true from the elaborate student registration packet to the fat three-ring binder explaining the board's procedures and practices.

Consistency is the gravitational pull that keeps all the planets of organizations, activities, and relationships in their proper orbits. But did this make the system at Xavier Prep inflexible or rigid? I never heard those words once during my visit. In fact, Sister Joan herself gave me a paradoxical explanation. "Consistency is the key—consistency and change," she declared. Before I could soak in how consistency and change could work together, she explained that the trust built up by relying on consistent processes and systems allowed for freedom to improve on those processes and systems. Sister Joan was describing a continuous improvement model of management built on her foundation of communication and community as well as consistency.

But exactly how does leadership bring about continuous positive growth? I decided to find Sister Joan's secret in my closing interview with her.

Level 5 Leadership

My last interview with Sister Joan included her taking the phone call I described at the beginning of this chapter. I was determined to explore with a surgeon's skill just what made Sister Joan's leadership so effective. She simply demonstrated it by stopping everything and taking a call from a hurting parent in the hospital and promising to "be there" for the ailing friend just as soon as needed. Sister Joan was the picture of servant leadership that the Bible describes and, I believe, Jim Collins defines. That leadership comes from caring more about the people you serve than about how you'll be appreciated or recognized.

I did probe further about Sister Joan's leadership style and perspective, but she summed it up best when I asked her simply what were the three things that she was best at. She replied, "One, I'm available." I thought back to her open door and the importance of communication at all the levels of the school. "Two, I delegate." Again I thought of the elaborate community structure where board members, administrators, teachers, parents and most of all students are empowered to achieve success. Then finally she said, "Third, I love this place." It's this last phrase, said with such genuine joy and delight, which explains the kind of consistency that can enable success.

Best Practices at Xavier College Preparatory

Level 5 leadership—demonstrated by Sister Joan Fitzgerald and her senior administrative team.

Separate men's and women's parent organizations—The Mother's Guild and the Dads' Club have unique programs for parent involvement and support of the students and the school.

Broad boards and committee leadership structure—Xavier has been able to harness the skills, abilities, and support of forty-seven board members through the effective distribution of Board responsibilities and active committees.

Effective development and program staff—The development department has been able to build a repeatable system for giving, including the annual fund, donor recognition, capital campaign, and fundraising events. Every staff member has a leadership role as well as a support role building tremendous esprit de corps.

Girls' Hope Home—A residential house for students who would be unable to attend Xavier either because of distance or family circumstances.

Well-kept campus and garden—Keeping the grounds (which include a magnificent rose garden) beautiful seemed to engender pride in the whole school family and a desire to take care of their school as well as one another.

Creating activities for every student—In addition to steering the students into the standard extracurricular activities and clubs, Xavier makes a concerted effort to create activities in order that each student might experience success.

Student assistance—A four-year program for mothers and their daughters covering issues such as eating disorders, self-defense, grieving and other life skills in preparation for college and life.

CHAPTER 9

Christian Worldview

How a Buzzword became the Backbone of the Curriculum

"Worldview, worldview, worldview—all I ever hear about is Christian worldview!" Amanda had attended only two days at her new school, Evangelical Christian of Memphis, Tennessee, and already she was fed up with hearing about this Christian worldview thing. She wanted her mother to know her displeasure. Fortunately that was years ago, and Amanda's mother was able to tell me the rest of the story.

After graduating from ECS, Amanda went on to attend a prestigious southern college. Her mother told me about how two Mormon missionaries visited Amanda's sorority house at the unwitting invitation of one of Amanda's sorority sisters. The missionaries spent two hours vigorously discussing and debating their faith. Amanda seemed to be the only one from the sorority who knew what she believed or could enter into the discussion. After the missionaries left, Amanda's sorority sisters gathered around. "How did you do that? How do you know all that stuff? I could never have carried on that conversation; it would have been over in five minutes!" Amanda's mother asked me if I knew what the reason was for Amanda's ability to articulate and defend her faith, but before I could respond, she answered her own question with a big smile: "Worldview!"

Christian worldview is a buzzword for many Christian schools, but at ECS it is the core around which the curriculum is built. Headmaster Steve Collums quotes Covenant College President Dr. Niel Nielson, who was a recent speaker on the ECS campus. Dr. Nielson began by using a standard definition of a Christian worldview as "seeing all of life in view of Christ." But Dr. Nielson went on to explain that "Christ needs to be seen as

Prophet, Priest, and King. Christ as Prophet reveals God's Word and truth, Christ as Priest reveals God's incarnational and gracious mediation in the affairs of all people, and Christ as King reveals God's Lordship over all of life." (See Appendix 5 for worldview resources.)

This more comprehensive understanding of a Christian worldview permeates the curriculum. Why? The answer starts at the top. Bryan Miller, president of ECS, quoted the latest survey from Barna that only 6 percent of born-again Christians have a Christian worldview. Bryan added, "This is our opportunity to fill a significant need in the Christian community." This is why ECS has recently added an academic mission statement: "The academic mission of Evangelical Christian School is to create a vigorous academic culture that kindles a passion for learning, develops intellectual gifts, and cultivates a Christian worldview so students are prepared for collegiate success and equipped to lead lives of integrity and influence for Christ." The teaching of a Christian worldview has become the core of the curriculum around which everything revolves.

Centering the Curriculum

The first step required to implement the academic mission was to find someone who would shepherd the project of aligning the curriculum to both teach and reflects a Christian worldview. Patrick Curruth, academic dean and chairman of the English department, was promoted to the post. After meeting Patrick and talking to him for a few minutes, I knew why he was selected. Smartly dressed with bow tie and jacket, he elicits the vision of a prep-school scholar, and his enthusiasm for the fulfillment of the academic mission is contagious.

Patrick was first given the task of developing a curriculum not for students but for teachers. The impetus for this teacher-centered curriculum was the belief that only when teachers know how to think "Christianly" about their subjects can they transmit a curriculum that truly reflects a Christian worldview. The result was a 25-hour class that all teachers must complete during their first two years of teaching. The course is a wonderful summary of how a Christian worldview contrasts with alternatives. It helps the teachers understand the building blocks of a Christian worldview. The final assignment is to either read Francis Schaeffer's book *How Should We Then Live* and respond to a list of questions or to summarize the lessons learned and explain their implications for the Christian school teacher in general and for the teacher and his or her subject in particular.

Having a teacher on campus who literally wrote the book on what the school wants its teachers to live by really helps Christian worldview to be a grassroots component of curriculum development. While this faculty study clearly gave teachers and administration a common vocabulary and process for developing curriculum, I was eager to talk to the teachers and students to see what really stuck.

Worldview Incorporated

I was pleased to get a rather random cross-section of teachers—the six teachers who didn't have a 7th period class. My question, "What did you think of Patrick's worldview class?" elicited the following comments:

"It gave us a common vocabulary."

"It freed me to be intentional in my teaching."

"It organized my thoughts."

"It integrated the sacred and the secular."

"It led me to the intentional pursuit of connecting curriculum with God's truth and making the connection for kids."

"We're actually applying our mission statement to practice."

"It helped but it's still tough to do in math!"

When I asked what difference it meant to their teaching, Brent, a history teacher, explained, "I'm able to give my students many hooks to hang things on. My students are able to make sense out of the flow of history."

Alan, a literature teacher, added, "My classroom is significantly better because all the literature fits together." Alan went on to explain that he used to teach literature the way it was taught to him at a secular university. Literature was just stories, each reflected upon by the random and subjective evaluation of the reader and various critics. This postmodern approach has been abandoned as Alan is able to study all of literature and its themes through the lens of a Christian worldview.

All of the teachers agreed that they believed that they were teaching their students to think. They all seemed to pick up the difference between education as the task of teaching students a fixed set of answers to a fixed set of questions as opposed to teaching students a way to process questions and be able to think and formulate meaningful and hopefully Christian answers.

The final test was the 7th period study hall students. Again I was able to interview a rather random group. When I asked what the students liked best about ECS, most reflected on their relationships with their teachers and friends. While this connectivity was number one, the character and quality of their education came in second. One student put it this way: "What I like best is the education; we're taught a worldview where Christ is infused into everything. Everything in the curriculum has to do with building our foundation." I think Patrick would have been very pleased to hear that.

Another component of the worldview emphasis is the faculty reading program. Over the past several years, faculty have read and discussed such works as Charles Colson's *How Now Shall We Live*, J.P. Moreland's *Love Your God with All Your Mind*, Richard Riesen's *Piety and Philosophy*, and Donovan Graham's *Teaching Redemptively*. Time has been set aside during in-service sessions for small group discussion. This has engendered a rich conversation that has produced not only a deeper understanding but also a broader appreciation of the Christian view of life and world.

ECS understands that none of this would work without the right teachers. (See "First Who, Then What" from chapter 3). When I asked Headmaster Steve Collums what he looks for when hiring a teacher, he identified two criteria. "First, an applicant must be a 'relater,' someone who loves kids, and second, a 'scholar,' one who loves the subject and commits to continuous study and growth. A teacher cannot impart what he or she does not possess." A school that can find teachers with those two qualities and give them the tools and training to teach from a Christian worldview will succeed in reaching its mission. And indeed, Evangelical Christian School seems to be well on its way to doing exactly that.

CHAPTER 10

The Flywheel at Work

An Example of a Teacher at Work

LYNDEN CHRISTIAN HIGH SCHOOL, LYNDEN, WASHINGTON

H ow would you like to have a teacher on staff who was named the Disney Teacher of the Year, the Busch Gardens/SeaWorld Environmental Educator of the Year, and was inducted into the Teacher Hall of Fame? Or how would you like the neighboring public schools asking if they could copy one of your curricular practices? These things all happened at Lynden Christian High School in Lynden, Washington. These accomplishments did not happen overnight, however. In fact, a visit to the Lynden campus made it clear that these successes took years to achieve.

When you walk up the steps to the school door, you notice white marble paving stones outlining the walk. Each stone is engraved with a year to represent each year the school has existed. Once you are inside the school you notice that a large picture frame including the senior pictures of each member of a particular graduating class is displayed along the front hall—one for each of the more than fifty graduating classes. A little farther down the hall you reach an atrium, which also serves as the vestibule outside the school's new auditorium.

The large cloth covering a 10 x 15-foot bulge in the wall just outside the auditorium piqued my curiosity. Someone explained that the large engraving underneath would be unveiled at the upcoming Grandparents' Day. It will depict three generations of Lynden students—a grandfather, his daughter, and his grandson, a current student. Next to the cloth is a large bronze plaque bearing the words of Psalm 78, that we are to pass on "the lessons from the past things...we will not hide them from our children, we will tell the next generation."

75

This little walk to the school offices gave me a glimpse of the value and stability of a strong heritage. The flywheel often takes many years to get turning. Lynden Christian has two shining examples of what can happen when you keep the flywheel turning.

Salmon and Science

Principal Keith Lambert introduced me to Harlan Kredit, the sixty-seven year old science teacher at Lynden, and asked if I would like to go with Harlan down to the stream where the school runs its own salmon hatchery. Keith didn't join us, although most school heads enjoy coming along on such tours. I soon realized that Keith may have declined because this "walk" turned out to be an aerobic workout. I practically had to run to keep up with Harlan.

We walked out the back door, down the hill, and past the track and football fields. I learned as we walked that Harlan is not only a science teacher but also the athletic director. He explained that Lynden hosts all the big public school track meets because it has the best facility in the country. Before I could ask how he finds the time to pull off such events, he explained that a team of 40 parents runs everything. Over his twenty-eight years as athletic director he has built organizational teams to run many of the athletic functions. I began to see how the flywheel is working at Lynden.

The organizational teams are composed of current and former parents, alumni, and boosters from the community. For football season, the "Chain Gang" calls Harlan and asks for the schedule, and volunteers take it from there. Harlan has crews for taking stats, announcing games, running concessions—every task you can think of. But all of this took time to develop. Recently I observed a brand new athletic director at another campus. The fellow served hot dogs in the concessions, had to find someone to fix the scoreboard, and finished up by putting away the sound system! What a contrast to Harlan's efficient teams.

Eventually we arrived at the fish hatchery. Inside the approximately 20 x 40-foot enclosed building was a long cement salmon run. Harlan told the story. Twenty-eight years ago he had returned to this community where he had grown up. He realized that the stream where he had fished as a boy was nearly dead. The lack of vegetation along the streambed, the pollution, and other factors had all but wiped out the salmon.

Harlan made a decision that shaped the educational opportunities for thousands of students over the next three decades. Harlan knew the project would take twenty-five years, but he was prepared to do what was necessary to restore this stream. While Harlan didn't know the terminology of the flywheel, he knew that it would take a long time to get it moving but that once spinning it could have transformational effects.

The first step was to plant trees along the streambed and attempt to hatch and release salmon into the river. That first year Harlan and his students experimented with hatching a few hundred salmon eggs in a rain barrel. Next they planted about 250 small trees along the stream. The flywheel was beginning to move.

Each of these projects grew so that now he and his students are planting approximately 2,000 trees each year and hatching thousands of salmon. These two projects have also spun off other projects as well. The school provides brochures for every 4th and 5th grader in the county explaining the need to be careful with the environment. The city of Lynden asked the students to put signs on all the storm drains in the city; all 1,400 drains now have notices reminding citizens not to pollute. The students have dug a channel for young fish to winter. The original project to spawn salmon eggs in a barrel has grown into ten large student-run projects each year.

Each of these projects costs thousands of dollars. Harlan explained, however, that the school has never spent a penny on any of the projects; in fact, he never even asked the school for money. The power of Harlan's flywheel is that it is making such a significant difference that it attracts the necessary money from the larger community.

These projects have been funded by city, county, and state monies and resources, service clubs, civic groups, national organizational grants, and donations from interested members of the community and school. Money has never been an issue. Rather than requiring and depleting resources, these projects have attracted greater and greater resources. As the projects have grown, so have the resources. The flywheel was spinning faster and faster.

But what about the students? Harlan began to tell their stories. One former student returned from college and now works for the very community organization with which Harlan originally partnered. Others have gone into careers in marine biology, fish and wildlife, and the sciences. This hands-on experience had inspired many students to further study and, more importantly, taught them that they could make a difference in life—because they already had.

Level 5 Leadership in the Classroom

My brief visit with Harlan made it clear that I was a witness not only to a great educator but to what Level 5 leadership can do at every level (see chapter 2). This is a lesson for all of us. Often we think Level 5 leadership is only a concept for those at the top of an organizational chart. But everyone must demonstrate leadership—the teacher in the classroom, the parent in the home, the worker with the new trainee. We all are leaders in some sphere. Harlan shows what that kind of leadership can produce.

When I returned to the school office, Keith Lamberts asked, "Did he tell you about his awards?" I recalled my conversation with Harlan and his words, "The kids do all the work," "My kids feel they own this project," "I have former students that walk around and see thirty-year-old trees that they planted and know that they can make a difference," "I get a lot of help from the other teachers." "What awards?" I wondered. Keith described the countless awards that Harlan has received, including the upcoming award as National Science Teacher of the Year.

No wonder the students want to work hard for this teacher, other teachers want to support him, and parents and alumni still ask how they can help. Harlan Kredit truly is an example of a Level 5 leader in the classroom—one who gives away all the credit and has the best for the institution and others at heart. This kind of leadership was needed to get the flywheel going in those early days with some salmon eggs in a barrel. It's this leadership that keeps the flywheel going today.

"May We Copy Your Presentations?"

While I was in the principal's office a call came in from White Rock Christian School. They wanted to observe Lynden's senior presentations. While it's always a compliment to have your peers want to observe and learn from your best practices, Keith explained that the "crowning achievement" for his senior presentations curriculum was when Mt. Baker Public High School called and asked permission to copy and implement Lynden's program.

Keith explained that this program took a lot of work over a period of time to get right. Seven years ago the State of Washington instituted the requirement for seniors to make a summary presentation prior to graduation. Faced with this mandate, the local consortium of the ten county high schools worked together on this project.

Lynden Christian School has been a good neighbor to the public schools in the consortium, but it has also benefited equally; in this case Lynden received over $50,000 of state money to work on its senior presentations project. When asked about the wisdom of working so closely with the public schools, Keith explained that he believes "the Christian school should be a transforming influence in the culture." Such an involvement is in keeping with the school's mission statement and purpose: "The mission of Lynden Christian School is to be an effective instrument of God. Together with Christian parents and the church, we seek to educate children and young people so that they may grow and mature into perceptive and caring Christians. Finally, our goal is to produce citizens *who have a transforming influence in the world*" (italics mine).

Lynden students are also required to compile a portfolio of work over their four years as high school students. While the portfolio project is still a work in progress, the senior presentations have been refined into a valuable component of the curriculum. The senior presentation program at Lynden is called the "Links Presentation." The title is a play on the name of the school's mascot, the lynx. But it is also a description of the presentation's goal, which is to link what the students have learned to who they are and where they are going. Each student is asked to make a 10–12 minute presentation. Students are granted a great deal of latitude as to what they can present and how they may present it. The goal is to encourage honesty. "We want the students to reflect, ask tough questions, and share their honest answers," explained Keith.

This is where the analogy of the flywheel comes in. Collins explains that for a long time one can be pushing on the flywheel without any perceptible movement. When the plan to implement senior presentations was first announced to the parents, Lynden's administration may have thought that the flywheel had rolled back over them.

"You're trying to pry into personal matters in our home." "You're forcing our kids to be phony." "It will take my child 600 hours to prepare for this new requirement!" The parents were angry, and they let the school know it at the first parents' meeting explaining the new requirement. The previous principal was questioning whether to throw in the towel, but the committee and the faculty as a whole had done their homework and knew that this would be good for the students and school. Had the criticism exposed unanticipated problems it may have been a different matter, but the school had good answers to the questions and criticisms, so they pushed ahead. Keith explained, "The program wasn't wrong—the perception was wrong."

I asked how they overcame the resistance. Keith told me the following story that he thought best described the program's early days. One family was particularly hostile. Two brothers who both had children in the school thought that the school was way out of line, wanted the school to pull the plug on the program, and loudly voiced their opinions at that first parents' meeting. The following year the brothers' father, the family patriarch, passed away. Soon after the whole family attended the senior presentation of one of the sons. In the student's presentation he wove together the story of his grandfather, his schooling, and who he was with the conclusion that he wanted to model his life after his grandfather's life. That night the student's father took Keith's hand and with tears in his eyes said, "This is the best thing that ever happened at this school."

While being stubborn when wrong can lead to disaster, staying the course when right can get the flywheel turning. Students, teachers, and parents told countless stories of meaningful senior presentations. Mike calculated exactly how many meals his mother had prepared for him and wanted to say thank you; Wendy did a liturgical dance when no one knew that was her passion and way of expressing herself; John, who had been bullied throughout his schooling, wrote a song and then explained how he had worked out the dissonance in his life; Damon started out his presentation, "I'm a nobody" and then went on to explain how he has dealt with his feelings and experiences in the reality of God's truth.

Like a giant flywheel, this program took extraordinary effort to get started. More than once the administration had considered abandoning it in the face of opposition. But just like the flywheel, over time and with constant pressure this program has become a hallmark of a Lynden education and has been part of the story of moving Lynden from good to great.

CHAPTER 11

Best Practices from the Business World

Applying Them to Christian Secondary Schools

CATHOLIC CENTRAL HIGH SCHOOL, GRAND RAPIDS, MICHIGAN

Brian, the school board chairman, sat down with the Executive Committee of the Board of Catholic Central High School in Grand Rapids, Michigan. He studied the yellow legal pad on the desk in front of him. Despite the school's 100 years of history full of wonderful landmarks and accomplishments, he and his board could not avoid the brutal facts outlined on that piece of paper staring at him:

Declining enrollment

Deteriorating buildings

Declining inner city neighborhood surrounding the school

- No athletic field adjacent to campus
- A campus bordered by a soup kitchen and mission

Increased competition

- One of the nation's top charter school companies is located in town and has a growing enrollment with their "free" flagship charter schools.
- State government is making significant funding commitments to public schools of choice.

Declining commitment of parents to private Christian education

Declining enrollment of feeder schools

Steve Passinault, a Catholic Central alumnus who began his career at Catholic Central several years before, entered the room. Steve had been recently appointed to the position of principal. His predecessor had been in the position only two years, and Steve was beginning to wonder if his leadership tenure would be equally brief. Brian, the school board chair, opened the meeting, "We have to do something now!" Steve knew Brian was right and had anticipated this moment.

"Brian, you're right, and quite frankly, the other senior administrators and I are not sure how to address these issues. We're not even sure where to start. We believe we need someone from the outside to make an assessment of this situation," said Steve boldly, wondering if he had just put his own job in jeopardy.

Brian said, "I'm glad to hear you say that, because we think this is exactly what we need. In fact, we're going to recommend an evaluation process that several of us have used in our businesses. It's called a SWOT analysis. The letters stand for Strengths, Weaknesses, Opportunities, and Threats."

Steve thought, "We all agree that we need an outside perspective but an assessment from the business world?" This was not what Steve and his staff had in mind. Thoughts flooded Steve's mind: "What could a process taken from the dog-eat-dog world of profit and loss have to do with the enterprise of shaping young lives? Can this possibly be a good thing? My teachers will never go for this." But then Steve realized, "The brutal facts point to a bleak future unless there is some kind of intervention. Maybe this strategy from the 'business world' is our best hope to right the ship. I guess we really don't have a choice."

Fast-forward five years to 2006. My research partner, Joe Chisholm, and I arrived at Catholic Central mid-morning in January. A late start had been declared because of the freezing rain, so we arrived before most of the students and staff. As we first approached the school we noticed a beautiful new academic wing. The landscaping creates a park-like quad at the center of a campus that speaks of excellence. The administration building is older, but Joe noticed that the polished floors in the entryway are so clean you could eat off them. We found our way to the office where Steve Passinault greeted us. In the next few minutes we heard about the growing enrollment, increased giving, minority scholarship program, newly integrated curriculum, and a new teacher evaluation process along with an increased focus on social responsibility on the part of the students.

What caused this transformation? It would be an oversimplification to say that it was merely the 2001 SWOT analysis. Certainly many, many people worked hard to make the changes necessary to get Catholic Central where it is today. But our investigation suggested that the SWOT analysis was the catalyst for this change. And this analysis model continues to be the driver behind the "Yearly School Management Plans." This chapter will narrate the use of a proven business practice as it was applied to a secondary Christian high school. We will then describe the results, including some best practices, that are exemplified by Catholic Central High School.

Benefiting from the Application
of Best Practices from the Business World

There has always been a tension between education and the business world. I remember in my early days as a young teacher wondering if "those board members" who seemed to all be from the business world really understood what education was all about. I didn't think that their business world insights would have much application to our school's enterprise. I couldn't imagine what reducing the error percentage part per million had to do with the art of teaching or how increasing productivity per hour on the line could equate to the time you needed to give to a struggling student who had come sobbing into your room at the end of a difficult school day.

But I have learned in the past twenty-five years (spent mostly in the business world) that this is a false dichotomy. Businesses have far more similarities with schools than differences because both rely heavily on human factors for success; principles that apply universally to these human factors are helpful in both settings. This is why best practices in people management, processing change, and personnel development have universal application in both the business setting and the school.

A more helpful dichotomy than "business world versus educational world" is described in a distinction that Michael Gerber makes in his best-selling book, *The E-Myth*. Here Gerber explains that a fatal flaw of most small businesses is that someone who is good at some particular skill or task concludes that they could make a living running a business in which they do that task or skill. The reality is that running a business requires a whole new set of skills and tasks that the artisan may or may not be good at—hence the subtitle of Gerber's book, "Or Why Four out of Five Small Businesses Fail."

What is the analogy for us? The teaching enterprise is like the artisan skill. This is why a gifted parent can homeschool a child and equal the academic success of an elite prep school. Running a school, however, is much closer to running a business than it is to teaching a child. The board member who has successfully run a large business has much to offer in running the business of the school but may have very little to offer in advising the teacher how to teach or the coach how to make better substitutions (especially when those decisions involve the board member's son or daughter).

The problem comes when we do not keep those two enterprises (teaching in a school and running the school) separate. At one of my first school board meetings, a board member complained to the principal that his daughter had not made the touring choir. Actions like that give boards a bad name. This board member had stepped over the line from advising the administration on the operations of the school's purposes, goals, and enterprise to interfering with a teacher doing her job. The business world would not tolerate board members who would show up on a work site and tell the electricians how to do their jobs. Gerber explains the difference between working *in* your business and working *on* your business. The solution here becomes attraction and retention of gifted board members who understand the difference between working *on* the business enterprise of the school rather than working *in* the school.

If we understand this distinction between the business of running a school and the art of teaching a student, then business principles have much to offer. Some may point out that even the business of school is different. This is true, but it's also true that every business is different. You won't run a school, a car dealership, or a factory all the same, but unless you take care of your employees and customers, all three will fail. While the products and corresponding processes may be totally different, the dynamics of the business enterprise have far more in common than they have differences.

Catholic Central's use of the SWOT analysis is an example of a practice taken from the business world and applied to the school. The SWOT analysis is often used when a turnaround is needed or new vision needs to be instilled. Some use it as an ongoing tool for long-range planning. First developed by the Stanford Research Institute in the 1960s, it was funded and developed by Fortune 500 companies who thought that their present long-range tactics had failed. The researchers interviewed 5,000 executives at 1,100 companies and organizations. Albert Humphreys, one of the originators, explains what they learned from their research:

> We discovered that we could not change the values of the team or set the objectives for the team so we started as the first step by asking the appraisal question, "What's good and bad about the operation... [both in] the present and the future?" What is good in the present is Satisfactory, good in the future is an Opportunity; bad in the present is a Fault and bad in the future is a Threat. This was called the SOFT analysis. When this was presented to Urick and Orr in 1964 at the Seminar in Long Range Planning at the Dolder Grand in Zurich, Switzerland, they changed the F to a W and called it the SWOT Analysis. (www.businessballs.com)

This tool has helped thousands of organizations in their corporate evaluation and planning processes. Let's see how it was adapted and applied at Catholic Central.

The SWOT Analysis Process at Catholic Central High School

A couple of ground rules were set up early. One was that the SWOT analysis had to be facilitated by a neutral, objective, and unbiased outsider. Board members and school administrators were too close, and the teachers still had a lot of apprehension. In this case the diocesan office that oversees the schools in Grand Rapids made the selection. The fact that this person was a gifted facilitator and perceived as truly neutral greatly assisted the process.

The first meeting, which lasted two and a half hours, began with the facilitator's explanation of the SWOT analysis. This was followed by filling in the four quadrants (Strengths, Weaknesses, Opportunities, and Threats) in three stages. First, everyone filled in the four quadrants individually on a piece of paper. Second, the facilitator collected the answers and put them up on an easel. Finally the group was asked to rank the significance of each item in each of the quadrants by voting. The top five issues in each of the quadrants were then identified.

Another priority was to ensure that all the stakeholders were represented. They were divided into five groups: faculty, support staff, board, general (including parents, students, alumni, etc.), and administration. This required scheduling of multiple meetings to make sure that representatives from each group could attend one of the meetings. The process went fairly smoothly, although one of the participants remarked that "it got a little tense when one of the weaknesses brought up is sitting two seats away from you." Other participants reflected that while it was satisfying to do the analysis, they were going to remain skeptical until they saw some tangible results. One tangible result began to take shape at the next two meetings.

At these next two meetings only two representatives from each constituent group were invited. The group took the top five threats and opportunities and matched them up with the corresponding top five weaknesses and strengths. (This is referred to as a TOWS matrix.) In other words, how do the external factors of threats and opportunities match up with the internal factors of weaknesses and strengths?

The results of working through the SWOT and the TOWS matrix yielded three priority items for immediate implementation. First was the need for greater integration and emphasis of Catholic social teaching in the school. This related to the number one identified strength—"a Christ-centered, faith-based, holistic approach to Catholic secondary education"—being applied to the number one threat, "decreased emphasis and value of Catholic secondary education among parents and church leaders." In other words, by building on the primary strength the school would be addressing the primary threat. By focusing on Catholic social teaching, which was seen as the most practical way to help students live their faith in the school and its community, they would be demonstrating the value of Catholic secondary education to those who were losing the vision. The win-win was that this also was driving the school back to its core mission and vision, which is summarized by the school's motto: "students you can have faith in."

The next two identified priorities dealt with weakness. First was the need for strengthening the marketing and recruitment of the school. This aligned the number one weakness with a host of opportunities as well as threats. Second was a call for better performance appraisal to deal with the third identified weakness: "incompetent employees, excess administration, and lack of evaluation follow-up." This lined up indirectly with a number of opportunities and threats but was also seen as very achievable.

Maureen Johnson, head guidance counselor at Catholic Central, reflected that no one had ever looked at weaknesses as opportunities but that doing so really tapped into people's creative abilities—instead of simply bemoaning the sad state of Grand Rapids' declining economy, they had to come up with original, creative solutions. Principal Steve Passinault pointed out that "one unexpected consequence of going through the process was achieving a broader base of funding for the school." The school had just completed a 16 million dollar capital campaign, which explained some of the new campus additions that Joe and I saw upon our arrival.

All of the administrators highlighted the need for teachers to buy into the process. They also praised the facilitator's ability to allow people to be heard without letting them turn the meeting into a gripe session. The process was also aided by faculty and staff reading *Who Moved My Cheese?*, an excellent book by Spencer Johnson about dealing with change. Let's take a closer look and see what the results of this SWOT analysis and TOWS matrix were.

Turning Threats and Weaknesses into Best Practices

Cindy Sielana explained that she was brought in to address an identified need from the original SWOT analysis. "We have always had someone recruiting, but adding marketing to my title has been a real change. We've had to make up most of the strategy ourselves." I asked her what the most significant success factors were in her role as head of recruitment and marketing. She identified five points: "First, you must have a marketing focus and budget—you have to spend the money to reach the kids. Second, you need to get your faith out in front! The next items highlight two of the school's real strengths. I always emphasize our school's high academic standards. Many colleges give our students a leg up in the application process. I also point out that our parent involvement is second to none. Our doors are always open, we have 'copy moms,' parent sponsors, parents who help on retreats, serve on boards—we want our parents involved. Finally, I talk about our scholarship programs for families with needs. We are also especially proud of our minority scholarship program where ten minority students in each of the four classes are given full rides."

I told Cindy that it's a wonderful sales pitch but asked how she closes the deal. Her answer revealed that she is just getting started: "I get them into MY school." I thought her use of the possessive adjective reflected her strong ownership not only of the school and its mission but her ownership of the sales and marketing process. Cindy continued, "I believe if I can get prospective students and parents into the school, it will sell itself. I make sure one of my student ambassadors takes the student on a tour or class visits. We have a Jr. Cougar program where we give junior high students a photo I.D. to get into special games. Before the student leaves the school I make sure that I have the student fill out a survey so I know where they stand.

"After the student has been on campus I call the parents and try to make sure that I'm working with them. I even challenge the parent and student to visit other schools. If they visit the local public school they will certainly see a difference. Last but not least I call everyone who doesn't register to see where they are at and if there is anything further I can do to encourage their enrollment."

Cindy's enthusiasm is contagious. The quality of her sales and marketing plan is worthy of a disciplined business setting. Cindy highlighted this point when she talked about her year-end evaluation process. "You've got to look inside the process every year; if you think you ever have it all figured out then you might as well close your doors."

The second weakness that the SWOT highlighted was the need to develop a better performance appraisal. I met with several teachers to discuss the new process, which includes not only standards but also planning for individual development and professional growth. The process also involves aligning all teachers who teach a particular class, including a common syllabus right down to a common final exam. I was talking to a long-time teacher who taught senior English, probably the top of the pecking order in most schools' English departments. She had just finished explaining the team approach to curriculum development and evaluation: "It takes time—time to meet, time to plan, and time to coordinate." I asked, "Why would a great teacher like you take all that time when you could just close the classroom door and go back to being a great teacher?" Her answer surprised me: "I found out that I wasn't as great as I thought. I've always been a very good literature and writing teacher, but the teacher who I'm teamed up with is very good at creative writing and poetry. I had put less emphasis there because these were my weak spots. Now with my teammate's help, I'm a stronger teacher and I've been able to help her as well."

The math teachers I talked to used the SWOT model at the departmental level. They also paid more attention to outcomes such as evaluating the results of P.S.A.T. testing and focusing on building their departmental goals.

When asked how the departments and teacher teams were able to overcome inertia and actually get started on the new evaluation process, many pointed to the principal's leadership. "Steve led by example. He met with us departmentally and helped us with getting started. His open door policy has reduced a lot of the resistance. Steve's personal involvement really helped. He showed us how to do it." Once again the critical power of leadership is significant, not only in the planning and evaluation phase but in the implementing phase as well.

The final SWOT goal was to integrate and focus on Catholic social teaching. Catholic social teaching refers to a specific set of principles that summarize the teaching of the Catholic Church concerning the responsibilities of a Christian living in the world today. The ten summary principles are human dignity, community and the common good, rights and responsibilities, option for the poor and vulnerable, participation, dignity of work and rights of workers, stewardship of creation, solidarity, role of government, and promotion of peace.

The senior religion curriculum was rewritten to integrate these principles. The first semester now focuses on the challenges of personal Catholic living; the second semester emphasizes social justice. The teachers work hard to make the curriculum penetrate the affective domain (behaviors) as well as the cognitive domain (understanding). As I discuss the creative assignments designed to help the student apply Catholic social teaching to life, I'm struck once again by the recurring theme of turning a weakness or threat into a strength or opportunity. I'm looking out the window at the soup kitchen and the subsidized housing project as the teacher explains the neighborhood tour and the encouragement for students to be involved in meaningful Christian service. I realize this campus location is an ideal location for Christian service and social responsibility, the very things that many Christian schools struggle to teach.

As our interview comes to a close I think back to an earlier conversation I had with the athletic director, Mike Neuman. Mike has been at Catholic Central for many years. He explained how he and his part-time assistant manage twenty-eight varsity sports with eighty coaches, including sixty-eight off-campus volunteers. He does this all in limited time and on a limited budget; he confessed his original fears that time and money spent on the SWOT analysis process would further deplete his resources. But he went on to say that now he was a believer. The success at Catholic Central meant growing resources and excellence for each department. So where exactly has this application of recognized business practices led? Mike's final words have stuck with me and provide a capstone for this narrative: "The thing that makes me feel the best is that we are living our mission. We're sending kids out into the world very well prepared for citizenship and adult life." I smiled inside; Brian and the entire board would have smiled, too.

CHAPTER 12

Law to Grace

How Transforming Student Discipline Transformed a School

LUTHERAN HIGH SCHOOL NORTH, MACOMB, MICHIGAN

Lutheran High School North's students had a reputation for being well behaved. For decades adherence to rules and proper behavior had been a hallmark of the school. As a young vice principal responsible for discipline, Steve Buuck had learned from the "best" disciplinarians.

Steve was taught to slam his keys on the desk for maximum effect as a student followed him into his office and then to slam the door so it made the pictures on the wall rattle—all to instill the proper amount of fear in the student about to be confronted, interrogated, or disciplined. The overstuffed chair that the student sat in was low and allowed the student to sink down into it. The intent, of course, was that the student should feel small and insignificant, leaving Steve with the "power position" in the impending confrontation.

Steve, a former football player and coach, had learned his lessons well. He wasn't afraid of military-style discipline and believed that he had benefited personally from some of the highly structured and disciplined environments he had navigated as he grew up.

Now, however, Steve wasn't following orders any longer; he was giving them. He had returned to Lutheran North after securing his doctorate in education and serving as football coach and dean at a Lutheran high school in Texas. He was now Dr. Buuck, principal of Lutheran High School North outside of Detroit. This day Steve had a disciplinary encounter with one of his students. He had used his old routine but just hadn't felt right about it. He tried to rationalize his discomfort, but he knew something was wrong.

The intercom on his desk interrupted his thoughts. "Dr. Buuck, Mr. and Mrs. Walters are here and would like to see you." Walters—the parents of the girl whom Steve had disciplined earlier in the day. Steve had dealt with dozens of upset parents when he was disciplinary dean, and now as principal he had already had one or two similar encounters.

What happened over the next few minutes transformed Dr. Buuck's perspective on discipline and as a result has transformed Lutheran North. The Walters, rather than coming in to attack, tried to understand what Steve wanted to accomplish with their daughter. Why had he treated their daughter the way he had? Their questions cut Steve. He really had no answers that he felt good about. Why had he treated their daughter with little or no respect? He knew the message that he sent was that conformity to a set of rules was more important than she was.

Steve struggled through the rest of the interview and thanked the parents for coming in with an open attitude and trying to help him and their daughter understand the goal of the earlier disciplinary encounter.

That night one question continued to haunt Steve. The parents had simply asked, "Why did you treat our daughter that way?" Steve had no answer. He knew that he certainly wouldn't want his own children disciplined that way. Late that night Steve resolved that things would be different when he returned to school the next day. He would first show respect for his students. Only then could he expect their respect and obedience for the school and its rules.

Over the past ten years Lutheran North has been transformed. Throughout my campus visit the concept of respect dominated. Lutheran North is still known for its well behaved students, but their behavior now comes from a heartfelt love and respect for their school. I heard evidence of this fact in almost all of my interviews.

From board members: "The teachers here are conveying respect for their students and we find that the respect is mutual."

From parents: "Parents are respected. We're invited to be part of the campus. We're always welcome." "I've heard Steve tell the faculty, 'We must let the students know that we respect them because if we don't respect them we can't expect them to respect us.'"

From teachers: "Dr. Buuck is the most amazing principal ever. He treats everyone with respect. He's a 'football guy' but he tells me he loves me. To have your boss love you is something I never experienced in the world of corporate training."

And from students: "The teachers give respect and they get respect in return. All the teachers show respect and they won't belittle you." "I feel respected. The teachers don't treat you like kids. You know that you're not on their level but they make you feel like you are."

As Steve concluded the story of his transformation he added, "I often go back to the Walters and thank them for showing me a better way."

But how did he, his administration, and faculty change the campus culture to one of mutual respect, or as Steve put it, one that went from law to grace?

Steps from Law to Grace
I wanted to find out exactly how this transformation of campus culture had taken place. Steve listed five steps that explained the change. I was encouraged that several of his steps echoed principles elaborated on earlier in this book. I was able to make a composite list of seven steps all together. The first two steps were supplied by my interview with the board.

The first step was leadership. The board member to whom we spoke recognized that the head of the school would not only need to model the school's mission but be able to implement it. Second, the right teachers and staff had to be hired. While this past year saw virtually no turnover in faculty, there had been large turnover in the early days of the transformation. The board members with whom I met explained that many of the teachers who had left were very committed, but that didn't mean that they were effective. "Their attitude toward students is the most important thing," he concluded. The school had committed to hiring teachers "who respect students." These first two steps are the foundation for greatness outlined in chapters 2 and 3.

The next five steps were supplied by Steve in our concluding interview. The third step was the need to, in Steve's words, "listen to your customer." This was essentially what Steve had done in responding to the Walters' questions. It also echoes the quality of so many strong school heads already cited in this study—being a good listener.

The fourth step involved focusing on the school's mission statement. Steve emphasized the importance of everyone owning the mission statement; in fact, he makes sure it is read at every faculty meeting. I reflected how much Lutheran High School North's mission statement exemplifies the hedgehog principle (see chapter 4). It reads: "Within our rich Christian tradition, Lutheran High School North is devoted to academic excellence and, above all, to sharing and modeling the Gospel of Jesus Christ in all aspects of its ministry by providing students diverse opportunities to serve their Savior while serving others." Steve concluded that in this step, it's very important to either "get on the train or get off."

The fifth step, which is an extension of the fourth, is the need for everyone to buy into the philosophy of discipline. One aspect of this is to focus on what the students are doing right. Steve believes that students are much better than their press and that the school needs to expect the best. "High schools that are well run have plenty of law because of the high expectations—that's why grace needs to be emphasized," said Steve. All must passionately own the mission and relentlessly drive it to completion.

I would have followed up with the obvious question about what happens when kids don't show respect and wander outside the rules, but teachers had already explained that to me earlier in the day. "Of course we have rules and consequences. That's the law, and students need to realize and face the consequences of breaking the law, but that's not the focus of the school," one faculty member had explained. "The focus is on forgiveness and restoration. We want the students to have the chance to start over." This was the gospel of grace that Steve had been teaching, and it seemed that not only the faculty but the entire staff had wholeheartedly embraced it. Steve explained that his lunch cooking crew had some of the greatest opportunities to witness to the students as they served. One of the maintenance staff had a significant ministry in modeling and working with kids. Everyone needed to own the philosophy.

The sixth step was Steve's hallmark: "Treat kids with respect." Even though this seemed to be the key transformational concept, it is interesting that Steve ranks it so low in order. I think this should be a reminder to each of us who would like to implement a best practice in our schools or our homes or our workplaces: there must be a basis upon which to build. The board could have called for a school culture of mutual respect, but without steps 1–5 in place, very little would have happened.

What does respect-based discipline look like? Steve believes it's discipline that comes not from coercion but from modeling respect for the student: "The kids I've disciplined know that I would get up in the middle of the night for them." The Scripture, I John 4:19, comes to mind: "We love Him because He first loved us." Steve lives that principle as he tries to model the concept of grace-filled discipline.

Step 7 is the need to keep raising the bar. Again this has been a characteristic of all our Growing Greatness schools, articulated in many different ways but with the same meaning: the need to continuously improve. This has led Lutheran North to a series of strong evaluation tools. In addition to the administration evaluating teachers, the school uses student evaluations of teachers as well. These prove to be a tremendously accurate barometer of what is going on in the classroom on a regular basis. Steve believes that master teachers really want and value these evaluations.

These are the seven steps that the school's leadership identified as leading Lutheran North from a climate of law to one of grace, a climate that displays a mutual respect for students and teachers, especially as it is reflected in student discipline.

The Fruits of Mutual Respect and Grace

While the focus on grace and mutual respect originally grew out of the need to redirect the school's approach to student discipline, I observed several unintended benefits of this new focus at Lutheran North. These were identified in chapter 6 as the byproducts of the flywheel's momentum.

First, there was the focus on respecting all learners. The concept of respect included special learning needs. As one board member put it, "Our special needs kids have respect." Lutheran North works very hard to accommodate all its students, including a deaf student and a wheelchair-bound student who was wheeled to the podium at the chapel I attended. The concept of respect helps the school to focus on each student's dignity, even when needs are different.

Another ancillary benefit was the fact that respect was extended to parents. The parents have become valuable members of the school team. Always welcome, parents have stepped up to help with administrative functions, running the Spirit Shop and bookstore, and serving on numerous formal and ad hoc committees. The parents we talked to shared a real enthusiasm for the school and its mission. One parent of a senior was so enthusiastic that she said, "I keep saying that we need to have another child so we can stay."

The search for respect led to a search to find a place for each student in the school. Teachers and staff look for ways to be involved that go beyond the numerous sports, clubs, and extracurricular opportunities. For example, each period three students help out in the office. This means that no calls go to voice mail during the day and the office always has plenty of help. The librarian is always on the lookout for library aides, which is really an excuse to help disciple a student who may not otherwise be involved. Teachers even mentioned that the custodial staff helps involve students. One student put it this way, "Being involved in something really makes a difference." He explained how teachers go out of their way to create opportunities for involvement, such as the recent addition of a chess club. The student exclaimed, "I actually went to a chess match, can you believe that? Me, at a chess match!" This support and mutual encouragement for each other is another fruit of a culture of mutual respect.

Finally I saw this respect growing into love. Too often we make the abstract feeling of love our goal. With concrete steps of right actions defined by the concepts of discipline and mutual respect, however, love can become a byproduct. Throughout my visit I heard board members, administrators, teachers, staff members, parents, and students talk about their love for their school family.

One of my interview sessions was with a group of students, all of whom had been suspended. I asked about their experiences. One student explained, "I did wrong. I was scared. I was suspended for three days. They brought me back in after the suspension. They told me, 'We still love you and want to put this behind you,' and they kept their word." A second student summed her experience up this way, "I've experienced forgiveness and Dr. Buuck has shown me how God would treat me." Our interview ended with these words from a junior boy. "I can trust Dr. Buuck; I know he loves me."

This is the transforming power of a well-run school with a Christian understanding of law and grace at work. As I concluded my visit with an exit interview with Dr. Buuck, he expressed his heartfelt conviction that Christian high schools are gifts from God to His church. It is easy to look at Lutheran North as just such a gift.

Appendix 1

Growing Greatness Survey Results

Each of the comprehensively studied schools was asked to have its teachers and administrators fill out the Growing Greatness Survey. The purpose of this survey was to ascertain how closely each school modeled the good-to-great principles that this book highlights. The survey was taken online using the popular web-based survey engine, SurveyMonkey.com.

The results of all the seven schools' responses are summarized below. It is hoped that the results of the survey highlighted below will help schools as they do their own self-assessment; they may wish to take the survey and to compare their own scores with the averages of the Growing Greatness schools. If your school would like to take the survey online, you can do so at cost (approximately $85) by calling the author of this study and survey, Dr. Gene Frost at 630-562-7516 or via email at gfrost@wheatonacademy.org.

The survey was divided into four sections: demographic information, questions about the head of school, questions about the school itself, and, finally, a number of short-answer questions. All the multiple choice responses are recorded here. The short answers were used in the study but are not shown here.

Demographic Information

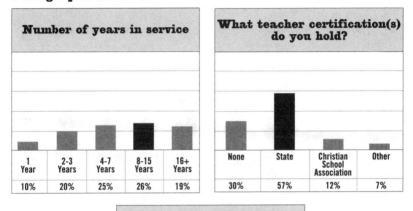

Number of years in service				
1 Year	2-3 Years	4-7 Years	8-15 Years	16+ Years
10%	20%	25%	26%	19%

What teacher certification(s) do you hold?			
None	State	Christian School Association	Other
30%	57%	12%	7%

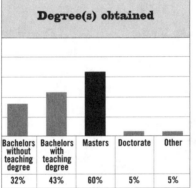

Degree(s) obtained				
Bachelors without teaching degree	Bachelors with teaching degree	Masters	Doctorate	Other
32%	43%	60%	5%	5%

Head of School Evaluation

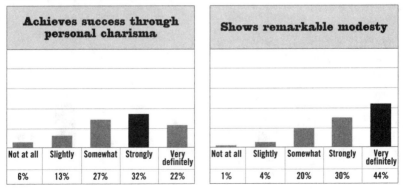

Achieves success through personal charisma				
Not at all	Slightly	Somewhat	Strongly	Very definitely
6%	13%	27%	32%	22%

Shows remarkable modesty				
Not at all	Slightly	Somewhat	Strongly	Very definitely
1%	4%	20%	30%	44%

A real workhorse

Not at all	Slightly	Somewhat	Strongly	Very definitely
1%	4%	19%	36%	41%

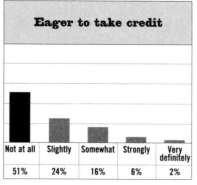

Eager to take credit

Not at all	Slightly	Somewhat	Strongly	Very definitely
51%	24%	16%	6%	2%

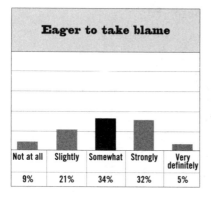

Eager to take blame

Not at all	Slightly	Somewhat	Strongly	Very definitely
9%	21%	34%	32%	5%

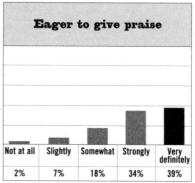

Eager to give praise

Not at all	Slightly	Somewhat	Strongly	Very definitely
2%	7%	18%	34%	39%

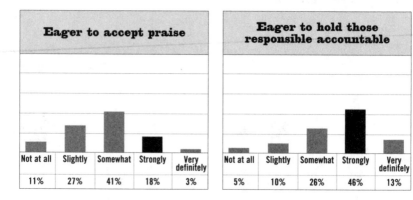

Eager to accept praise

Not at all	Slightly	Somewhat	Strongly	Very definitely
11%	27%	41%	18%	3%

Eager to hold those responsible accountable

Not at all	Slightly	Somewhat	Strongly	Very definitely
5%	10%	26%	46%	13%

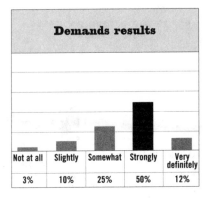

Demands results

Not at all	Slightly	Somewhat	Strongly	Very definitely
3%	10%	25%	50%	12%

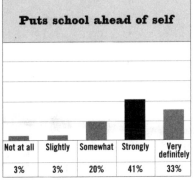

Puts school ahead of self

Not at all	Slightly	Somewhat	Strongly	Very definitely
3%	3%	20%	41%	33%

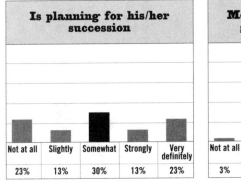

Is planning for his/her succession

Not at all	Slightly	Somewhat	Strongly	Very definitely
23%	13%	30%	13%	23%

Motivates by holding up goals and principles

Not at all	Slightly	Somewhat	Strongly	Very definitely
3%	7%	17%	37%	36%

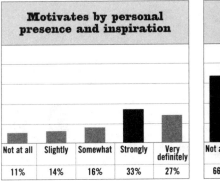

Motivates by personal presence and inspiration

Not at all	Slightly	Somewhat	Strongly	Very definitely
11%	14%	16%	33%	27%

Blames others, external factors, factors out of his/her control

Not at all	Slightly	Somewhat	Strongly	Very definitely
66%	19%	8%	6%	1%

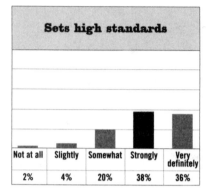

Sets high standards

Not at all	Slightly	Somewhat	Strongly	Very definitely
2%	4%	20%	38%	36%

Stays the course no matter how difficult

Not at all	Slightly	Somewhat	Strongly	Very definitely
4%	6%	14%	47%	30%

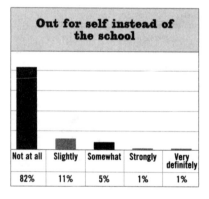

Out for self instead of the school

Not at all	Slightly	Somewhat	Strongly	Very definitely
82%	11%	5%	1%	1%

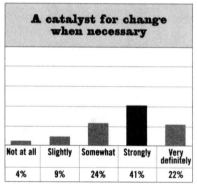

A catalyst for change when necessary

Not at all	Slightly	Somewhat	Strongly	Very definitely
4%	9%	24%	41%	22%

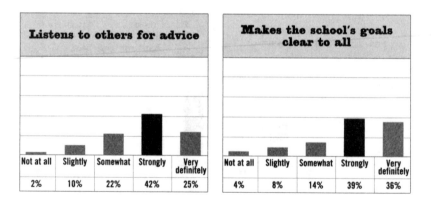

Listens to others for advice

Not at all	Slightly	Somewhat	Strongly	Very definitely
2%	10%	22%	42%	25%

Makes the school's goals clear to all

Not at all	Slightly	Somewhat	Strongly	Very definitely
4%	8%	14%	39%	36%

School/Teacher Evaluation

Hiring and retaining great teachers is absolutely critical to mission

Not at all	Slightly	Somewhat	Strongly	Very definitely
3%	6%	16%	32%	44%

Great goals and standards are absolutely critical mission

Not at all	Slightly	Somewhat	Strongly	Very definitely
1%	4%	8%	38%	49%

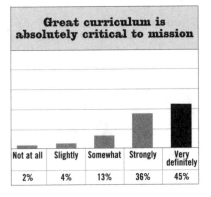

Great curriculum is absolutely critical to mission

Not at all	Slightly	Somewhat	Strongly	Very definitely
2%	4%	13%	36%	45%

Achieving great results with students is absolutely critical to mission

Not at all	Slightly	Somewhat	Strongly	Very definitely
1%	4%	11%	44%	41%

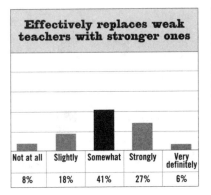

Effectively replaces weak teachers with stronger ones

Not at all	Slightly	Somewhat	Strongly	Very definitely
8%	18%	41%	27%	6%

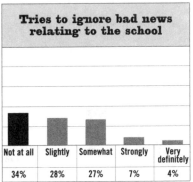

Tries to ignore bad news relating to the school

Not at all	Slightly	Somewhat	Strongly	Very definitely
34%	28%	27%	7%	4%

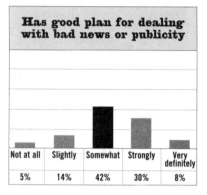

Has good plan for dealing with bad news or publicity

Not at all	Slightly	Somewhat	Strongly	Very definitely
5%	14%	42%	30%	8%

School deals with difficult decisions head-on

Not at all	Slightly	Somewhat	Strongly	Very definitely
5%	13%	25%	38%	19%

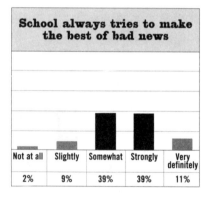

School always tries to make the best of bad news

Not at all	Slightly	Somewhat	Strongly	Very definitely
2%	9%	39%	39%	11%

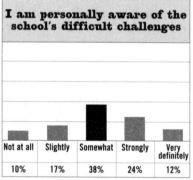

I am personally aware of the school's difficult challenges

Not at all	Slightly	Somewhat	Strongly	Very definitely
10%	17%	38%	24%	12%

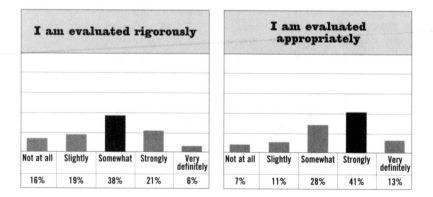

I am evaluated rigorously

Not at all	Slightly	Somewhat	Strongly	Very definitely
16%	19%	38%	21%	6%

I am evaluated appropriately

Not at all	Slightly	Somewhat	Strongly	Very definitely
7%	11%	28%	41%	13%

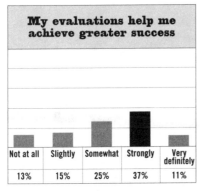

My evaluations help me achieve greater success

Not at all	Slightly	Somewhat	Strongly	Very definitely
13%	15%	25%	37%	11%

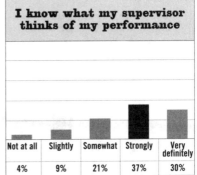

I know what my supervisor thinks of my performance

Not at all	Slightly	Somewhat	Strongly	Very definitely
4%	9%	21%	37%	30%

Clear performance measures track our school's success

Not at all	Slightly	Somewhat	Strongly	Very definitely
5%	13%	34%	34%	14%

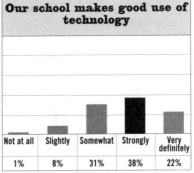

Our school makes good use of technology

Not at all	Slightly	Somewhat	Strongly	Very definitely
1%	8%	31%	38%	22%

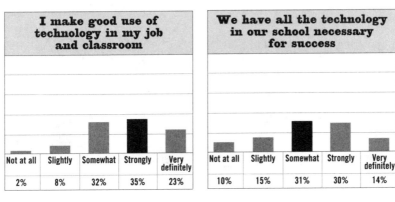

I make good use of technology in my job and classroom

Not at all	Slightly	Somewhat	Strongly	Very definitely
2%	8%	32%	35%	23%

We have all the technology in our school necessary for success

Not at all	Slightly	Somewhat	Strongly	Very definitely
10%	15%	31%	30%	14%

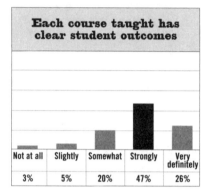

Each course taught has clear student outcomes

Not at all	Slightly	Somewhat	Strongly	Very definitely
3%	5%	20%	47%	26%

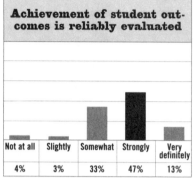

Achievement of student outcomes is reliably evaluated

Not at all	Slightly	Somewhat	Strongly	Very definitely
4%	3%	33%	47%	13%

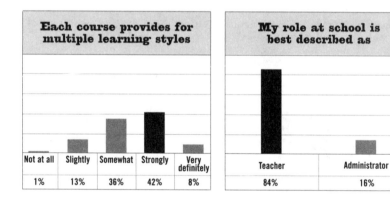

Each course provides for multiple learning styles

Not at all	Slightly	Somewhat	Strongly	Very definitely
1%	13%	36%	42%	8%

My role at school is best described as

Teacher	Administrator
84%	16%

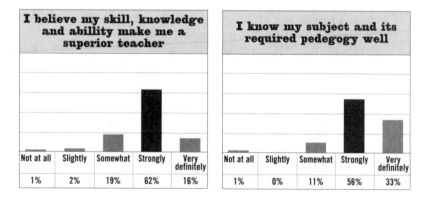

I believe my skill, knowledge and abillity make me a superior teacher

Not at all	Slightly	Somewhat	Strongly	Very definitely
1%	2%	19%	62%	16%

I know my subject and its required pedegogy well

Not at all	Slightly	Somewhat	Strongly	Very definitely
1%	0%	11%	56%	33%

I am very confident in my ability to control my class

Not at all	Slightly	Somewhat	Strongly	Very definitely
1%	2%	6%	56%	36%

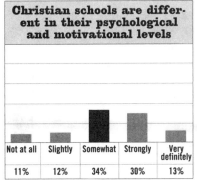

Christian schools are different in their psychological and motivational levels

Not at all	Slightly	Somewhat	Strongly	Very definitely
11%	12%	34%	30%	13%

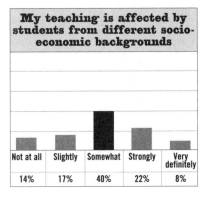

My teaching is affected by students from different socio-economic backgrounds

Not at all	Slightly	Somewhat	Strongly	Very definitely
14%	17%	40%	22%	8%

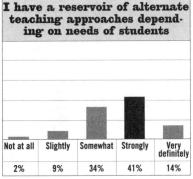

I have a reservoir of alternate teaching approaches depending on needs of students

Not at all	Slightly	Somewhat	Strongly	Very definitely
2%	9%	34%	41%	14%

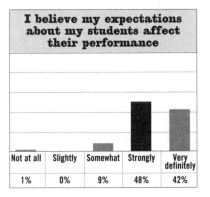

I believe my expectations about my students affect their performance

Not at all	Slightly	Somewhat	Strongly	Very definitely
1%	0%	9%	48%	42%

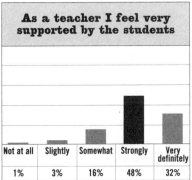

As a teacher I feel very supported by the students

Not at all	Slightly	Somewhat	Strongly	Very definitely
1%	3%	16%	48%	32%

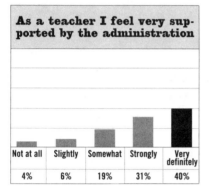

As a teacher I feel very supported by the administration				
Not at all	Slightly	Somewhat	Strongly	Very definitely
4%	6%	19%	31%	40%

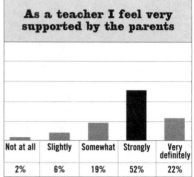

As a teacher I feel very supported by the parents				
Not at all	Slightly	Somewhat	Strongly	Very definitely
2%	6%	19%	52%	22%

As a teacher I feel very supported by fellow teachers				
Not at all	Slightly	Somewhat	Strongly	Very definitely
1%	1%	10%	48%	40%

Appendix 2

Level 5 Leadership Evaluation Summary

Chapter two discussed the concept of Level 5 leadership. Each education-al leader in our seven comprehensively studied schools was asked to do a self-assessment based on the leadership grid contained in Jim Collins' book *Good to Great*. This same assessment instrument was then given to a small sample of teachers and administrators. The results of the survey are below.

Not surprisingly, the scores the leaders gave themselves in general are lower than the scores given by those who evaluated them. This reflects, presumably, the humility of a Level 5 leader who is genuinely able to give away the credit for his or her accomplishments. Schools may find this survey helpful to use in some form in the leadership evaluation process.

Respondents were asked to rate each of the eight characteristics* on a 1-5 scale (1 being "not at all" and 5 being "absolutely Level 5"). This summary has been slightly altered to better fit the school setting rather than the corporate setting.

Professional Will	Head's Self-Evaluation	Administrators' Evaluation	Teachers' Evaluation
Creates superb results, a clear catalyst in the transition from good to great.	3.4	4.0	4.2
Demonstrates an unwavering resolve to do whatever must be done to produce the best long-term results, no matter how difficult.	4.0	4.3	4.5

*eight items modified from the list generated by Jim Collins in his book, *Good to Great*, p. 36

Sets the standard of building an enduring great school; will settle for nothing less.	3.6	4.4	4.5
Looks in the mirror, not out the window, to apportion responsibility for poor results, never blaming other people, external factors, or bad luck.	4.4	4.2	4.3
Personal Humility			
Demonstrates a compelling modesty, shunning public adulation; never boastful.	4.0	4.6	4.8
Acts with quiet, calm determination; relies principally on inspired standards, not inspiring charisma, to motivate.	4.6	4.5	4.7
Channels ambition into the company, not the self; sets up successors for even greater success in the next generation.	4.2	4.4	4.3
Looks out the window, not in the mirror, to apportion credit for the success of the school— to other people, external factors, and good luck.	4.6	4.5	4.3

Appendix 3

Included in the study was a customer satisfaction survey provided by SureVista of Lansing, Michigan. Dr. Richard Spreng, associate professor of marketing at Michigan State University, developed this survey as a way to apply some of the best practices from the business world to Christian education (see chapter 11 of this book for other examples of applying business best practices to schools).

We are all familiar with customer satisfaction surveys, and many Christian schools do survey their students, parents and constituents for constructive feedback. The genius of the SureVista report is that it not only asks how well is a school doing in a given area but how important that area is to the parent. This two-dimensional grid tells a school not only where improvement is needed but what are the most important areas to focus on from the parents' perspective.

While the two-dimensional reports are only helpful to the individual school, we have included a summary of the overall satisfaction scores for seven Growing Greatness schools. Grand Rapids Christian High School was substituted as our seventh school to create our seven-school average.

If your school would like to take the survey you can contact SureVista at:

> *www.surevista.com*
> *241 E. Saginaw*
> *P.O. Box 800*
> *East Lansing, MI 48826*
> *800.990.7202*

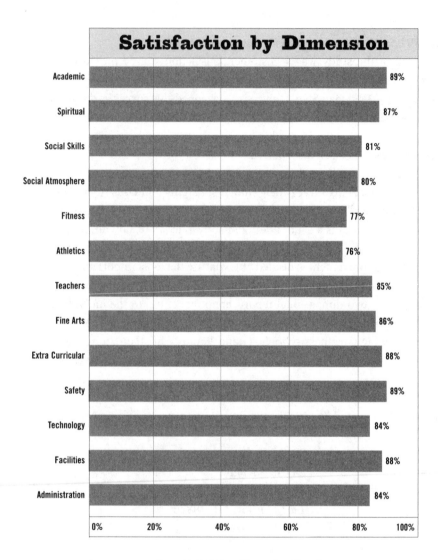

Satisfaction by Dimension

Dimension	Percent
Academic	89%
Spiritual	87%
Social Skills	81%
Social Atmosphere	80%
Fitness	77%
Athletics	76%
Teachers	85%
Fine Arts	86%
Extra Curricular	88%
Safety	89%
Technology	84%
Facilities	88%
Administration	84%

*percent responding with 7, 8, 9, or 10 on a 1 to 10 scale

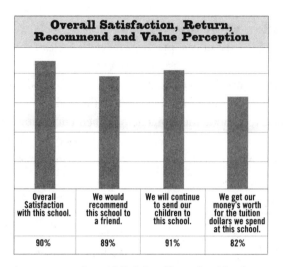

Overall Satisfaction, Return, Recommend and Value Perception			
Overall Satisfaction with this school.	We would recommend this school to a friend.	We will continue to send our children to this school.	We get our money's worth for the tuition dollars we spend at this school.
90%	89%	91%	82%

*percent responding with 7, 8, 9, or 10 on a 1 to 10 scale

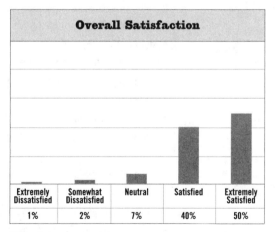

Overall Satisfaction				
Extremely Dissatisfied	Somewhat Dissatisfied	Neutral	Satisfied	Extremely Satisfied
1%	2%	7%	40%	50%

*10-point scale conversion:
Extremely Satisfied=9 or 10
Satisfied=7 or 8
Neutral-5 or 6
Somewhat Dissatisfied=3 or 4
Extremely Dissatisfied=1 or 2

Appendix 4

Best Practices of the Growing Greatness Schools

The following is a list of best practices the author gleaned from his study of the Growing Greatness schools. This is not meant to be an exhaustive list but rather a catalog to highlight some good practices of Christian schools. It is hoped that some of these ideas might inspire other schools to include these practices in their curriculum. These lists might also inspire a school to build its own list of best practices in hopes of improving and sharing these practices with others.

Comprehensively studied schools	Best Practices
Annapolis Area Christian School 109 Burns Crossing Road Severn, MD 21144	• Use of facilities as a revenue source • Honor code and student prefect board • Senior projects • Mentoring groups • Dress code using uniforms • Model for college advisement—meet with every student before senior year • Institutional Community Service and Stewardship • Institutional Advancement and Capital Campaign: AACS has moved from a part-time development person to a staff of six professionals who work to advance the school's mission through support for faculty programs, student financial assistance, capital campaign efforts, publications, and endowment growth. Use of tax-exempt bonds, foundation support, planned giving, and alumni involvement have all been essential to the school's growth.

Comprehensively studied schools	Best Practices
Bellevue Christian High School 1601 98th Ave NE Clyde Hill, WA 98104	• Curriculum collaboration—English and history departments collaborate on a major research paper • Appeals process encouraged up the chain of command • Philosophy for dealing with Christian families, not merely Christian students • Sports innovations—i.e. "families in the locker rooms after games"
Cincinnati Hills Christian Academy 11525 Snider Road Cincinnati, OH 45249-1218	• J term • S.O.S. program—student led service program • Technology in the classroom • Dance Program (full-time dance instructor)
First Presbyterian Day School 5671 Calvin Drive Macon, GA 31210	• Fundraising—from wrapping paper sales to professional development program • Impact of hiring curriculum director • Blue Ribbon school • Making best use of public resources (using Junior College labs, etc.)
The King's Academy 8401 Belvedere Road West Palm Beach, FL 33411	• Chapel class— students plan and lead chapels • "Capturing Kids' Hearts"—Flip Flippen's program, social contracts • Outside advice (Paideia, Inc.; SWOT analysis) • Prefect system instead of student government • Rotation schedule—different class schedule each day

Comprehensively studied schools	Best Practices
Westminster Christian Academy 10900 Ladue Road St. Louis, MO 63141	• Accessibility for all families—work with special learning needs • Sport pillars—principles that guide the sports program • Senior service projects • Modified block schedule
Wheaton Academy 900 Prince Crossing Road West Chicago, IL 60185	• Project L.E.A.D. / Project Serve (Zambia/World Relief) • Winterim—creative 2 ½ week program between semesters • Living curriculum teachers—recruit and train the best
Schools studied for Best Practices	**Best Practices**
Catholic Central High School 319 Sheldon Ave Grand Rapids, MI 49503	• Maximizing inner city location • Minority scholarship program • SWOT analysis planning tool
Evangelical Christian School P.O. Box 1030 7600 Macon Road Cordova, TN 38088	• Worldview class for teachers • Presidential model of leadership for school head • Model fundraising program and campaign
Lutheran High School North 16825 24 Mile Road Macomb, MI 48042	• Theme for the year • Student office help • Grace-focused discipline based on respect • A place for every student (including all staff in program)

Schools studied for Best Practices	Best Practices
Lynden Christian High School 515 Drayton Street Lynden, WA 98264	• How to partner with public schools • Senior presentations • Empowering teachers to succeed (Harlan Kredit)
Xavier College Preparatory 4710 North 5th Street Phoenix, AZ 85012	• Student Assistance—Four-year program for mothers and their daughters covering issues such as eating disorders, self-defense, grieving and other life skills in preparation for college and life. • House for disadvantaged students (Hope House) • Broad boards and committee leadership structure • Focus on extracurricular involvement for each student

Appendix 5

Worldview Resources

The following is a brief list of some of the resources available to those attempting to teach from an explicitly evangelical worldview. As pointed out in this book, it is no longer possible to teach only a Christian/non-Christian dichotomy. We must equip our young people to evaluate the many diverse philosophies to which they will be exposed in modern culture.

These resources are designed first of all to help a student understand a Christian worldview and then to supply the student with the tools to evaluate the alternative lifestyles, philosophies and entertainment options that they will eventually encounter. At the close of this section is a challenge for Christian educators as to what might be the next step in integrating Christian worldview training into a thoroughly Christian education.

A Sampling of Worldview Resources

Diehl, Steven. *What's Wrong with My Christian School—Exploring Christ, Culture and Purpose.* Richmond, VA: Steven Diehl, 2007. [This book is available by contacting the author, c/o The Veritas School, 6627 Jahnke Rd., Richmond, VA 23225; 804-864-2123]

Dockery, David S., and Thornbury, Gregory Alan. *Shaping a Christian Worldview.* Nashville, TN: Broadman, and Holman Publishers, 2002.

Greene, Albert E. *Reclaiming the Future of Christian Education.* Colorado Springs, CO: Purposeful Design Publications, 2003.

Harris, Robert A. *The Integration of Faith and Learning.* Eugene, OR: Cascade Books, 2004.

MacArthur, John, Mayhue, Richard L., Morley, Brian K., and Tatlock, Mark A. *Think Biblically: Recovering a Christian Worldview.* Wheaton, IL: Crossway Books, 2003.

Noebel, David. *Understanding the Times.* Eugene, OR: Harvest House Publishers, 1994.

Plantinga, Cornelius. *Engaging God's World: A Christian Vision of Faith, Learning, and Living.* Grand Rapids, MI: Wm. B Eerdmans, 2002.

Poe, Harry Lee. *Christianity in the Academy.* Grand Rapids, MI: Baker Academic, 2004.

Sire, James. *The Universe Next Door.* Downers Grove, IL: Intervarsity Press, 1997.

Stronks, Gloria Goris, and Blomberg, Doug. *A Vision with a Task.* Grand Rapids, MI: Baker Books, 1993.

Wilhoit, Jim. *Christian Education and the Search for Meaning.* Grand Rapids, MI: Baker Book House, 1986.

Wolterstorff, Nicholas P. *Educating for Life.* Grand Rapids, MI: Baker Academic, 2002.

Organizations

Nehemiah Institute; www.nehemiahinstitute.com
Summit Ministries; www.summit.org
Worldview Academy; www.worldview.org

Teaching and Learning from a Christian Worldview—

A proposal for the next step

BY KORI HOCKETT

While there are many resources on the topic of Christian worldview, they are focused on the philosophical attempt to define a Christian worldview as compared to a variety of other worldviews and to lay out the theoretical and philosophical principles of a Christian worldview that should be applied to teaching. The task of teaching what makes a worldview Christian as compared to naturalism, existentialism, nihilism or any of the other major worldviews has been laid out clearly by authors like James Sire, Robert Harris and David Noebel to name just a few. Others, like David Dockery, Gregory Thornberry, Albert Greene, Gloria Stronks and Doug Blomberg have begun to apply those principles to Christian education. Almost all of the resources explain principles like creation, the fallen state of mankind, redemption, the primacy of Scripture, the notion of reality, the ultimate purpose of all people, and their importance and foundational importance in Christian education.

What does not seem to be thoroughly exposited is the practical application of a Christian worldview to the various disciplines taught in a Christian high school. One key principle that has begun to emerge is the unity among faith and learning (Dockery and Hornbury, p. 81). The phraseology of "integration" is somewhat of a misnomer as we truly affirm the unity of all truth (p. 81). However, as educators who wish to reveal that unity, we need to begin to bridge the gap between the philosophical dimensions of worldview study and the practical teaching that occurs in the classroom. The dangers of staying at the philosophical level could be extremely damaging to students as they would be exposed to "proof-texting" of the principles of a Christian worldview, which would not necessarily be in context as they are taught in a particular discipline.

Also, it is important for students to be able to live out their knowledge and beliefs in their everyday lives, so while understanding that Christians must know reality based on the perspective of God as the Creator is important, we must also help students apply these types of principles to practical living.

One potential solution to the application and execution of teaching students to think biblically is to study and determine what Scriptural principles emerge from each discipline and emphasize one particular principle in each discipline. This is not to say that teachers would exclude all other opportunities to "reveal" the connections between faith and the discipline, but they would focus on one particular Biblical principle that especially relates to the discipline. This would give teachers a focal point to emphasize in their curriculum rather than overwhelming teachers with the task of revealing all of the connections between faith and their discipline.

This program would allow Bible departments to function as the overarching structure for teaching students key principles like creation, the fallenness of man, redemption, the primacy of Scripture, the notion of reality, and the ultimate purpose of all people. The application of this teaching would then occur in each discipline. A sample program might look like the following:

In the math department, all classes would focus on the principle of absolute truth and the order that is instituted in God's creation.

In the science department, all classes would focus on the implications of Psalm 24:1-2, "the earth is the Lord's and everything in it." The overarching principle would deal with the creation and God as the Creator.

In the English department, all classes would focus on the power of the Word (referencing John 1), and the idea of the Word that became incarnate flesh to communicate truth to the world. Classes would also deal with the importance and value of language, which would allow a treatment of the primacy of Scripture as God's word to us.

In the foreign language department, all classes would focus on the principle of "love thy neighbor as thyself" (Leviticus 19:18). If we are to love our neighbors, we must be able to speak their language, understand their culture, and be able to communicate effectively with them. This is the primary reason to study other languages and cultures, as greater understanding would lead to a greater ability to communicate the Gospel.

In the social studies/history department, all classes would focus on the principles laid out in Zechariah 7:9-10, which deal with justice, the treatment of the poor, and evangelism.

In the business department, classes would focus on the principles dealing with money and stewardship (Matthew 6:24).

In the technology and computer science department, the foundation would come from 1 Corinthians 10:23-24 that "everything is permissible but not everything is beneficial." This would allow the discussion to focus on human capability through technology coupled with the ethical questions of the benefits of that capability.

In the fine arts department, the emphasis would be on beauty and meaning (Psalm 104). As artists students would have the ability to communicate God, his truth and his glory by bringing meaning to ordinary experiences. These emphases would "awaken us to God's nearness, deepen our awe, love, praise and service to him (Greene, p. 134).

In the physical education department, all classes would focus on the principle that we must use our bodies for purposes of righteousness (Romans 6:18). This would also relate to helping students apply the principle that our bodies are a temple (1 Corinthians 6:19) to practical living.

By creating a singular focus for each discipline that is informed by Scripture and obviously relevant to the material, teachers would be able to reveal the unity of faith and their discipline in a more practical way. Students would get the big picture in their Bible classes and see the microcosmic picture in each of their disciplines. While this plan is still very much a work in progress, it is an attempt to take the next steps in teaching from a biblical perspective and ensuring that students not only have knowledge about their Christian worldview, but can use that knowledge in practical ways for the furthering of God's Kingdom. As educators, our task is to take the philosophy and the foundational principles and bring them to life for our students in the classroom. Then, we will be one step further in our attempt to truly educate the "hearts and minds" of our students according to God's truth.

Kori Hockett is a history teacher and curriculum coordinator at Wheaton Academy in West Chicago, Illinois